NEW
Decorator's
Handbook

N E W
Decorator's
Handbook

JOCASTA INNES

B🌾XTREE

First published in Great Britain in 1995
by Boxtree Ltd,
Broadwall House, 21 Broadwall,
London SE1 9PL

Text © Jocasta Innes 1995

All rights reserved

The right of Jocasta Innes to be
identified as Author of this work has
been asserted by her in accordance with
the Copyright, Designs and Patents Act
1988

1 3 5 7 9 10 8 6 4 2

ISBN 0 7522 1650 3

Special photography and artworks ©
Paint Magic Jocasta Innes 1995
Designed by Hammond Hammond
Special photography by Lucinda Symons
and Mark Gatehouse
Styling by Sarah Delafield Cook and
Timna Rose
Illustrations by Kate Simunek

Repro by Jade Reprographics Limited,
Essex
Typeset by SX Composing Limited,
Rayleigh, Essex
Printed and bound in Glasgow by Bath
Press Colour Books

A CIP catalogue entry for this book is
available from the British Library

ACKNOWLEDGEMENTS

It is only fitting that my first book to bear the Paint Magic logo should reflect the enthusiastic teamwork which is the company's operating style. This project cut across job descriptions: everyone piled in with ideas, experience, painting and styling. Creative chaos needs management, and we were lucky to conscript Alex Artley, honorary team member: to her go the thanks of the whole crew. Thanks also to Sarah Delafield Cook, our pocket marvel, who drove the project from start to finish in so many different capacities: writing, planning, painting and styling (it is a surprise she has not grown six sets of arms like the goddess Kali). I am grateful to decorative painter Tom Lane for sharing his extensive knowledge, to Angeles Blasco for her insight into colour and its uses, and to Dawn Reader who led the team on site, with a brush rather than a baton; ably assisting her were David Faulkner, joiner and designer, and Lee Mulligan, Chloe Potts and Joanna Livingstone who are all talented with a paint brush. On the publishing front my thanks go to Michael Alcock, who launched the concept, Penelope Cream, who edited the book, and to Roger Hammond who designed it.

Lastly, many thanks from us all to the proprietors of The Blue Door and Graham & Greene for lending props and furniture.

Contents

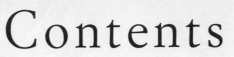

INTRODUCTION

*P*AINT BRINGS OUT the child in us – the free, creative side of every human being which is often submerged by day-to-day life. Decorating our home is one part of adult creativity that gives great and lasting pleasure. Thinking about colour, light, space and mood is a wonderfully private, domestic act that no one can take away from us. However we earn a living, a can or two of paint, carefully chosen, can alter a room beyond recognition, transform a battered object such as a sturdy, beloved old chair or mirror and give us the chance to recast the "spell of home".

We now have a tendency to forget about the elaborate dragged, ragged and stippled effects of the past with all their associations of expensive antique furniture and luxuriant old textiles. Instead, the new look is younger, fresher, and direct. Colour washes give the fresco-feel, being warm, comforting and matt, and they provide a sense of water-based purity. Whether we actually live in town or country, we like the idea of simple rustic finishes, plain, honest furniture, or the witty, child-like directness of vivid colours and possessions, carefully chosen but deliberately pared down to the minimum.

Young homeowners now have a new confidence to demand and expect more of the do-it-yourself home-improvement market. Much of this has come from the introduction of high-street "style houses" selling attractive and durable interior accessories at an affordable price. Technological successes in the manufacture of ready-to-use paints and glazes have also moved the emphasis away from the challenges of mixing the correct formulas to concentrating instead on the versatility of paint and on the richness of colour itself.

For a successful interior simplicity is the answer; one or two good, strong colours combined with simple shapes will guarantee clarity of design (left).

Approach colour combination adventurously. Colour can radically alter the way you feel about a room and the things you do in it.

The new interest in paint has a lot to do with the rural traditions of the poor, "making do" in traditional simplicity. This could be stark, Shaker-influenced rooms, a well-trodden tiled floor instead of lavish close-carpeting or the comfortable clutter of an English country cottage in which the prettiest bits of china sit on a colourwashed mantelpiece high above the kitchen stove. To accompany these images, we think of the yellow of buttercups, the old green of thyme or of glossy, rich olives, baked earth and the orangey-pink of terracotta or the cloudy grey-blue of lavender. All this tends towards the relaxed, natural atmosphere of a welcoming home.

Home is the ultimate good place and here the possibilities of paint are endless. Apart from the fact that it is the cheapest way to transform an interior, it is also the most satisfying in that it can be used, quite magically, to unify and harmonize rooms and objects with amazing ease. It is also a quick way to indulge one's imagination and to express individuality. In just one coat any mood can be created, from the warmth and intimacy of

Pretty, delicate motifs have been applied to this stool using transfer paper, a very helpful material for those who are not confident of their free-hand drawing skills.

glowing geranium pinks to the classic sophistication of forest greens and classic blues. But it is not just colour that can bring about your desired mood, but the actual application of paint. While a patchy, colourwash effect will create an informal and friendly environment, a bold and rigid stripe will give dignity and order to a room. Paint is only surface deep and its effects are the means of artifice, but the power of colour and painted texture on the human sensibility cannot be underestimated.

This book has two aims. At the beginning we start with materials, equipment and preparation and share the technological developments that have come about since the 1980s. These have produced some quite revolutionary products that will enable you to take many short cuts. Secondly, it will give inspiration to the home decorator, and to the newcomer in particular, and prove just how easy and what fun it is to experiment. For this reason the decoration projects were carried out in a one-bedroom apartment occupied by very busy (and impatient) students. With these rooms came all the typical challenges that many homeowners or tenants inherit. It is beginners who bring reality to an area that is often at risk of becoming indulgent and whimsical, with their questions on every-day decorating dilemmas: is there anything to be done with outdated, 1960s' laminated kitchen units? What about miles and miles of white gloss woodwork? Is there any alternative to dreary frosted glass? Well, there are answers to all these problems, and the story of how these four rooms were transformed soon demonstrates how far reaching the possibilities of paint can be. I do not pretend that just by reading about techniques you will become an expert overnight but with the helpful hints and some invaluable short cuts I hope to give you a good start.

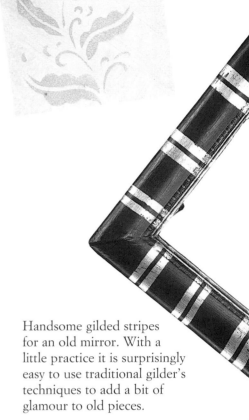

Handsome gilded stripes for an old mirror. With a little practice it is surprisingly easy to use traditional gilder's techniques to add a bit of glamour to old pieces.

Walls need strong colour to create warmth

Need extra shelving

Bright colours for cupboard See mondrian painting

Unit to be painted, if possible?

Pull up carpet

What about a distressed effect?

STARTING OUT

EFORE YOU DO anything at all, ask yourself this question: why you are decorating? Is there some urgent task to address or is it just a hobby? Are you decorating because the room has great potential and day-to-day life in it is going to be vastly improved, or is it because you want to increase the value of your home for re-sale? If it is the latter, then remember that inappropriate decoration schemes, or interiors that have been given dubious modernization, are often the last to shift on the property market.

Let's assume that the room shows great potential and ask the next question: how much time should you allow, or, rather, how much time do you have? Never be seduced by the glossy images in magazines or do-it-yourself videos and think that decorating is a neat and tidy affair – it isn't. If not carefully planned and the right amount of time allocated, decoration can be one of the most disruptive activities to family life. If you have small children, do not try to tackle everything at once, but take one room at a time. Everyone needs a sanctuary to escape to at moments like this. A thorough reading of the next chapter will help here and so too will a good appreciation of the importance of preparatory work. In the professional world it is the standard of preparation for walls, furniture and woodwork that separates the good finished job from the mediocre.

Your rooms

The real key to success is to recognize your limits. Or more importantly, the limits of your rooms – with good instruction, the right equipment and enough confidence, a beginner can aim for the top. In terms of proportion, look hard at your room, try to see it as a shell and analyse what you have. Take note of the shape and size of the room, the door and window design, niches or alcoves and applied architectural ornament such as moulding or cornicing or other plaster work. If there are restrictions (for instance too high a ceiling in a small room) and you do not want to incur the expense of structural work, try to see this as an interesting challenge and be encouraged that the right colour or technique can resolve problems quickly. On the other hand, if you feel you do not have any problems in these areas, do not make the mistake of thinking you have complete freedom to choose any effect. Size and proportion should always be one of the determining factors when choosing a colour and technique, as should the amount of light. An inappropriate choice can quickly destroy the sense of order and balance.

Sometimes, inheriting too much ornament can be a problem. The Victorians were particularly enthusiastic when it came to aggrandizing their interiors. Few surfaces could get by without an adornment of tiles, panels and knobs. However, if these features are not to your taste, and you feel they interrupt the mood, rather than removing them altogether use paint to soften and disguise them. *Original features should be shown respect* and, often, they are the one thing that appeals to future buyers. If, on the other hand, you have a modern box-like interior to which you would like to add a little character, it is best to limit yourself to a few trimmings such as simple moulding or cornicing, or baseboards (skirting). Mismatched or crude imitation features will quickly destroy any hopes of achieving elegance or harmony.

Once irregularities have been taken into consideration it is then a good idea to concentrate on any advantages and

walls must be sanded down

Old glass on fireplace needs sanding and priming

room needs a picture rail

needs to distract eye from boarded-up grate

good floor boards, make something of them?

Green paint must go!

window needs softening with a fabric - muslin?

Needs central feature here

Decorate with motifs - blues greys

floorboards in good condition, Scandinavian effect?

Needs some thing for privacy, paint effect on glass?

Warm, earthy colours for walls, perhaps Terracotta?

Put mirror glass, in picture frame

Pipes to be painted out

Old lino to be removed

capitalize on them. In the rooms described later, the job was made easier by the lack of modernization but some problems did arise. In the kitchen, there was a nicely sized window but also some rather dull and very dated laminated units. In the sitting room there were quality wooden floor boards and generous baseboards (skirtings) but the absence of a picture rail exaggerated the height of the ceiling. The ways in which these particular problems were dealt with are described in later chapters, but the point here is that paint must be considered as both the key for hiding weaknesses as well as the ingredient that can emphasize the advantages of a particular room.

FURNITURE

The other thing to consider before work begins is, of course, the furniture. It is best to have as firm an idea as possible on the final choice of pieces. It is easy if you have only a few items to deal with but for the less fortunate who have accumulated vast quantities over the years it is best to steel oneself, be ruthless and get rid of those pieces that only add clutter. Try to take into account the activities that are to go on in a particular space and do not concentrate only on aesthetically pleasing arrangements. A room that looks sensational is nothing if it is not comfortable. At the same time, do not be afraid of empty areas – the eye needs relief, particularly if the paint effects are lively. It is the odd gap that adds serenity and calmness to the overall scene.

INSPIRATION

Even with a long-cherished plan that you want to put into immediate action, it is still wise to have a look at the ideas the latest magazines are offering. Dipping into them can re-affirm your tastes or alert you to a useful new product. If you simply do not know what your taste in interior design actually is, the most useful exercise is to look through some interior design books or magazines and try to pin-point exactly what it is that appeals to you. You will find that more often than not it is the colour. As explained in Chapter 2, it is colour that will have the most impact on the eye and which will create a profound emotional affect. Whatever your financial means, good colour is the one thing that you can have. The myriad ranges of both historical and contemporary paints, as well as quite brilliant mixing machines and useful recipes, mean that you really can obtain what might once have been just an elusive effect that appeared only in your dreams.

After consulting the colour advice in Chapter 2, it can also be helpful to visit your local art gallery and see what the real colour magicians have done. The Fauvists were always experimenting with complementary colour and the Pointillists with optical mixtures. The Romantics were experts at exotic and sensual colour and the Conceptual artists with bold and sparkling primaries. Best of all is to see the use of colour in domestic context. Visit historic houses and see what combinations past generations have come up with. In England the Bloomsbury group offers some quite startling but very successful ideas from their base, Charleston, in Sussex. For help in all areas of design the Victoria and Albert Museum in London's South Kensington houses one of the best collections of historic wallpapers, fabrics and furniture, and also has complete room sets showing how these were put together.

Jot down your ideas, collect swatches, cut-out pictures and postcards, and lay them all out and see what you have. Move them around, add and subtract. Use our designer's colour boxes in the Decorator's Organizer to record these and then, on reading Chapter 4, decide on your plan of action.

This vivid green combined with gold is a bold and original choice. For colour inspiration visit your local art gallery to see what colour combinations artists have used over the years.

COLOUR

NORMALLY SIGHTED PEOPLE rarely notice it, but we are bombarded by every hue and tone in the spectrum each day. Very often it is young children who see primary colours with startling clarity. Usually, we only notice colour in a fresh way when Nature taps us on the shoulder and says, "Hey, look at this!" That could mean a rainbow arching through rain and sunshine or the moment at which, on reaching a new holiday destination, we are struck by the blue of the sea or little pink- and yellow-washed houses on a dry, cracked hillside.

But colour is not only the artist's terrain. It has been studied scientifically for centuries as a branch of physics (optics). For decorative purposes we do not need to go into the science of colour too closely but, as we show here, a traditional colour wheel is the most logical way of expressing the full range of colours at our disposal. Basically, all colours belong to a family and each family progressively blends with the next.

Consult a colour wheel to discover which colours complement each other.

Colour behaviour

Like people, colours work together or reject each other according to certain basic rules. This is called **colour behaviour**. Whatever colours are chosen in a decorative scheme, the ultimate aim is to achieve what is known as a "settled effect". If this is not done, the room will be psychologically uncomfortable to spend time in.

Here, so-called **complementary colours** such as red and green, or crimson and lime-green, or blue and orange, must be used with particular care. If, say, two complementary colours such as red and green are given equal weight in a decorative scheme, the human eye will not be able to focus on them simultaneously and the result will be an unpleasant flickering sensation which no amount of soft furnishing or the pleasing arrangement of pictures or decorative objects will be able to correct. (To see the disturbing optical relationship between red and green, stare hard at a red dot on a white piece of paper and then stare hard at a plain white piece of paper. You will see a green dot float there as an "after-image".)

When using complementary colours, one colour must be allowed to dominate fully and its partner possibly used to "spike up" the scheme in a small but telling way. For example, in a blue room orange might be used on cushions or on pretty china, but a little of this goes a long way. "Complementary" is, in fact, not a very good word to describe certain pairs of colours. "Opposites attract and repel" might be a better way of expressing the effect.

The behaviour of colours also involves a feeling of depth or the illusion of space in a room because some colours naturally advance while others recede. Red, for example, always "advances" and, when used solidly on all four walls, will make a room appear smaller. To see the truth of this in Nature, look at red geraniums from a short distance away. The flowers will

Use colour cleverly to create an appropriate mood for each room. Rich terracotta creates comfort and warmth for this quiet reading room (left).

Deep reds, pinks or shades of mulberry can make a large, high-ceilinged room feel friendlier and more intimate. You can increase this feeling with collections of small prints and paintings.

always appear to be closer to you than the green leaves which cluster around them. Red is therefore an ideal colour to use to draw together an uncomfortably large, bleak room, particularly one in which you have little furniture, a dining room perhaps.

Blue, violet, greeny-blue and black make walls appear to recede and, when used solidly in a small room there is a sense of "drawing away" to the distance, and of spaciousness. As in the case of red too, the use of these colours depends to a great extent on what natural light is available in the room. In a sunny south-facing room, cool colours can look refreshing and achieve the desired effect of spaciousness without bleakness.

Bright yellow (a current decorating favourite) always attracts the eye and, if you like it, it is a marvellously versatile and friendly colour. The Chinese preferred it as a colour against which to display porcelain (a fact not lost in many traditional English country house Yellow Rooms) because it is the only colour in the spectrum which positively enhances or projects every other colour in the spectrum. The exact yellow, however, must be carefully chosen to achieve this effect and should verge towards the redder yellows. A greeny-yellow will look unpleasantly slimy and liverish by both sunlight and artificial light and shades verging towards mustard will not retain the useful effect of "projecting" and "holding" other coloured objects. Yellow is obviously a very good background colour on which to add stencilled decoration because it is almost impossible to apply an unsuccessful stencilled colour combination.

Green usually comes across as a neutral "floating" or meditative colour but one which needs particular skill in pairing with other colours. White and cream used to be thought of as the great colour "easy options" but nowadays they have become the basis for very sophisticated decorative schemes based on

If you are careful and ensure that there is some relief for the eye, you can just as easily throw together several bright colours as you can pastels (right).

The combination in this entrance hall of rich, earth colours such as reds, ochres and terracottas provides a very warm welcome for visitors.

A subtle combination of blues for this kitchen manages to be vibrant without being cold (above).

These walls have been given a coat of cool, blue limewash, a traditional paint made from slaked lime, water and pigment that allows the walls to breathe with its slightly chalky, porous finish (left).

Dark blue stripes create a masculine and gently formal effect for this bedroom.

layering lots of objects and textiles of the same neutral colours – white on white, cream on cream. Curiously enough, this idea has an ethnic basis. The anthropologist Margaret Mead found that the Inuit had 17 different words to express the colours of differing snow conditions.

How colour behaves in interior decoration can be defined to some extent by science and by the cumulative experience of professional interior designers. But in the end, it also comes down to personal taste and feeling and this is where you step forward. The most beautifully achieved room in the pages of a glossy magazine will not do a thing for you or your domestic peace if the colours simply do not appeal to you. The **psychology of colour** is of overwhelming importance and cultural background plays its part here. The most obvious example is the reversal of the symbolism of white and black between Chinese and European cultures. Wear white in China and you are in mourning. Wear it in Christian Europe and you are a bride.

But in the main, the psychology of colour has a fairly universal personal application. If you are doubtful about your own colour preferences, the following checklist might be useful:

■ Look at the colour wheel on p.19. Do you prefer warm colours or cool ones? Unless you live in an enormous house where you have the luxury of space for experimenting with different colours, the chances are you will not naturally veer towards both types.

■ Which colours do you actively dislike? Certain colours have unpleasant associations for some people. If eating too many oranges made you sick on a school bus, you may loathe orange for evermore. Did you once recover from an operation in a room painted eau-de-Nil? You may associate pale green with hospitals ever after.

■ Any colour associations? Many people think they have lucky colours. From childhood onwards we may have "comfort colours" associated perhaps with a grandmother's kitchen in

Violet is traditionally associated with mystical qualities. This bedroom is certainly uncompromising in its colour choice but remains imaginative and fun.

Pale yellow is a good choice for providing warmth for large rooms without destroying the feelings of light and space (above).

Soft yellow with pale grey is a classic combination and can be found in many historic European houses. Here, the colours have also been picked up in the curtains and upholstery (right).

Broken colour effects, such as the colourwashing, add an extra dimension of luminosity and depth to wall decoration (far right).

which we were particularly loved and welcome, or a favourite outfit, holiday or toy.

■ What is the room to be used for? Bold colours really do stimulate conversation which is fine in a sitting room or dining room but would you really want a tremendous amount of talk in a bedroom?

■ What aspect does the room have? A room facing north will never enjoy strong sunshine and, unless you are emotionally fixed on cool colours, something warm would definitely lift the tone of the room and give it welcoming warmth.

■ Do you work from home? A study room or office in the house or apartment might stimulate you best when painted in bold, strong colours, leaving you free to exploit more restful colours in the leisure part of your home.

■ Does the room contain a large, fixed, coloured object which you are going to have to work around? This could be a big green-tiled fireplace, a bright blue wood-burning stove, or an expensive carpet or sofa you cannot afford to replace just yet.

■ In one room do you long for a luxury feel yet you are on a modest income? You do not need lots of antique furniture and china to enjoy colour schemes with a luxurious feel. Emerald green has been a colour of opulence since the late eighteenth century when the chrome yellow used to mix it was first chemically stabilized. Used with gold and white, it was Napoleon's favourite colour scheme. Purple is also a colour associated with luxury, used by Roman emperors and rock kings. Pure cream and white schemes since the days of decorators like Syrie Maugham, Elsie de Wolfe and Basil Ionides have suggested Modernist luxury. Ultimately, it suggests that you can afford to keep everything utterly spotless (even if you have to do it yourself).

■ Does the room have a negative feature you wish to disguise with colour? Unsightly pipes are best blended in with dark colours; if very high ceilings make you feel adrift in a room, a darker colour than that used on the walls will give them the

impression of being lower than they are. On a more personal level, we must now come down to the more intimate psychology of colours – what it means in your innermost psyche.

In the early twentieth century, Dr Max Luscher, Professor of Psychology at Basle University devised a colour test to reveal personality traits. The Luscher Colour Test is still seen as a useful tool of enquiry into emotional states:

■ YELLOW Indicates an active, spontaneous, adaptable and creative personality. Primitive life was sharply divided into night and day and bright yellow indicates the action and energy of hunting in bright sunshine.

If you prefer the qualities of spaciousness and light that plain white walls provide, use pieces of painted quality furniture as a way of introducing some of your favourite colours (above).

Some shades of green are thought to be cold, yet when combined with the warmth and texture of old woodwork can create a fresh but homely environment (previous page).

■ DARK BLUE Primitive people associate this colour with the starry night sky, sleep and security. If you like it, it indicates a relaxed, tender and affectionate personality.

■ RED There never seems to be any doubt about the interpretation of this colour. A preference for it associates you with excitability, sexual drive, extroversion, the will to dominate and impulsiveness.

■ GREEN As this colour is the "negative" partner of red, it indicates stubbornness, tenacity and deep conservatism.

■ VIOLET Indicates mystical and aesthetic qualities and also some degree of emotional immaturity.

White on white is a great favourite with some designers. Investigate historical paint ranges for different shades of white. These tend to be softer and more subtle than the usual brilliant white offered in high street stores.

■ BROWN Said to be preferred by people in need of physical comfort and tenderness.

■ BLACK Decorative schemes based on this colour are often alarmingly sophisticated. A strong preference for it indicates a personality in a state of resignation, renunciation or revolt.

■ GREY Indicates an indecisive personality in a state of feeling uncommitted or unresolved.

In the end, if you are still undecided about colour after thinking through these promptings, one of the best ways of resolving colour schemes in a room is simply to copy, on a large scale, an existing colour scheme which already works attractively on a small object you are particularly fond of. Painted china and textiles provide some of the most beautiful and original colour combinations to be found anywhere – the Mediterranean, Scandinavia, the Middle East or our own traditional rural art. If you own a particularly beautiful multi-coloured plate, rug or bowl, your best bet might be to base an entire room scheme on it.

The most important thing about colour (after choosing it) is to mix it very carefully. Enough paint for the entire room should be mixed at one time as batches are almost impossible for an amateur to copy. Colour mixing is a delicate art in itself and you may need to practise a little. But in the end, if you make a bad mistake with colour – either in choosing it or mixing it – there is one very good thing you can say about paint: even the most brilliant decorators have usually made one huge mistake, if not more, in the course of a professional lifetime. Should that happen to you and it is a case of hue and cry, remember that within a few weeks, a bit wiser in the ways of colour, you can always pick up a brush and begin the magic all over again.

A room based on a clever combination of neutral tones and natural fibres. This room manages to be cool and elegant as well as comfortable (left).

If you feel you need very pale or white walls to obtain the maximum amount of light for small rooms, use paintings and prints to provide colour and interest instead of a decorated wall surface.

3

LIGHTING

*L*IKE PLANTS, we are "phototropic". We are fascinated
by light and find ourselves drawn towards it, just as
moths on a warm evening are drawn towards a
flame. Like a vase of flowers or some good
pictures, light spells civilization – it draws us into a room and
completes the psychological mood that the colours we have
chosen have already begun to create.

Although the human eye can rarely see it at first, artificial
light provides its own subtle sources of colour. Ordinary,
tungsten-filament light bulbs produce a very yellow, warm effect
in comparison with natural daylight in all seasons. The new
energy-saving bulbs produce a slightly paler yellow light.
Fluorescent tubes produce a bluer, cooler light and, even in the
kitchen, this light is not very welcoming. Spot lights and flood
lights give a whiter, brighter light in a strongly focused
direction. Table or standard lamps in soft-coloured shades give
colour depth to a room, with silk shades acting as the most
gentle diffusers of artificial light.

Light can also be used to create "light patterns" in a room.
Do you wish to throw light up or down? In a broad arc or a
narrow one? Well-chosen lighting can intensify the optical
illusions you have already begun to achieve by using colour to
give the impression of altering the dimensions of a room. Low
pools of light on side tables can create a wonderfully intimate
effect in a high-ceilinged room where the ceiling is left unlit. On
the other hand, putting a wash of light over a low ceiling will
make a low, enclosed room seem bigger and higher.

Considerations

Badly thought-out lighting can cause fatigue, distraction, boredom, stress and, at the very worst, accidents. When planning a room there are several different lighting purposes to be considered:

TYPES OF LIGHTING

■ **General lighting** Every room needs one general, central light which can be switched on instantly in moments of emergency or just for simple reasons of better visibility such as when doing the cleaning.

■ **Task lighting** This is the level of light needed to perform a given task such as reading, writing or sewing. It varies according to your eyesight and can only be decided upon by personal experimentation.

■ **Mood lighting** This is the psychological effect you wish to produce, usually after dark, in the sitting room, dining room and bedroom, to enhance the decorative scheme. Here, coloured shades can be used to intensify or add sparkle to the colour you have already chosen. For the emotional effects of coloured light, look again at the psychological effects of colour given on pp.27-35.

■ **Accent lighting** This is a way of highlighting particularly beautiful objects such as pictures, sculpture or a group of interesting plants (plants respond best to uplighting) which can provide a focus for particularly interesting textures, colour or form. Lighting of this kind also draws attention away from dull parts of the room or from pieces of furniture which, although useful, you may be stuck with because to replace them would be too expensive.

■ **Information lighting** This particularly applies to stairs and landings and is needed to avoid accidents in dangerous areas.

■ **Security lighting** This applies to driveways, garage doors and points of criminal access. If in doubt as to whether a particular door or area is in need of security lighting, consult your local police or a security firm.

1 Mood lighting Lamps at a low level are one of the best ways of producing gentle, atmospheric light.
2 Accent lighting A way of creating a pool of light from above with a recessed ceiling spot.
3 Concentrated lighting An adjustable spot secured on a track provides concentrated illumination.

INDIVIDUAL ROOMS

No decorative scheme comes alive until it has been subtly lighted and here your imagination can come into play, particularly in the sitting room, dining area and bedroom where there is the greatest potential for mood lighting. Here is a quick guide to what you should consider in various rooms:

■ **Sitting room** The greatest variety of lighting may be needed in this room because from day to day you may well be watching television, reading or entertaining your friends with music and good talk. This is the principal place to consider carefully positioned pools of light from table or standing lamps positioned in relation to the furniture.

■ **Bedrooms** Dual-switch lighting that can be operated from both door and bed is particularly handy here. You will also need bedside lighting for each partner to read in bed and lights for the dressing table; you may also consider installing lights which will come on automatically when you open the door of a deep cupboard, closet or wardrobe.

■ **Bathrooms** Safe lighting is the most important consideration here. Fixtures must be enclosed and switched on either from the outside or by a pull-cord. Lights around a mirror or built into a mirror-fronted cabinet are also essential, plus task lighting for the bath and shower area. If you are at all dubious about fixing lighting fittings in a bathroom, it is best to seek expert help.

■ **Kitchen** Casting unwanted shadows as you stand at work surfaces is the biggest lighting problem in the kitchen. Consider whether you are likely to block light from a central fitting when working at the stove, sink or side surfaces. Would carefully placed spot lights solve the problem? Or would fluorescent or strip lights under wall cupboards create a good after-dark cooking environment?

■ **Dining area** Here the lighting is mainly for the table and the people eating and talking around it. A dimmer switch is a good idea; it can be used to lower the amount of light in the room to provide just the right ambience for candles on the table.

An interesting way of incorporating an uplighter into the architectural features of a room. Be careful that one doesn't diminish the qualities of the other.

■ Halls, stairs and landings Good, warm light in a hall provides a bright welcome and can make a small hallway seem sophisticated and attractive. On stairs and landings, light should be positioned so that shadow falls either across the treads or across the risers, so that each step can be identified easily. The shadow of the walking person must not destroy the contrast between the planes.

When desiging your lighting scheme make sure you take into account all the activities that will be taking place in the room rather than concentrating on the ambience alone (left).

This is the most functional way of looking at lighting but, in creating an interior, never forget that lighting fixtures themselves should look good in both their daytime and after-dark roles. From dramatically modern to exquisitely antique, in metal, glass, plastic or wood, light fittings can add exciting shape and colour to a decorative scheme.

The master glass craftsmen Emile Gallé and Louis Comfort Tiffany recognized the decorative value of lighting fixtures at the beginning of this century when electric light was coming into widespread domestic use. Inspired by natural forms such as mushrooms, palm leaves, tulips and drooping flower heads, they unleashed the power of coloured glass in fantastic shapes and varying sizes from chandeliers to small nightlights.

For those on a budget, candle light is still the most beautiful way of making people feel special in rooms where you receive visitors. Massing candles on a simple mantelpiece against the magic of a mirror creates an atmosphere of deepened colour, peace and happiness which even the most sophisticated lighting system cannot reproduce.

Spot lights can be used to create pools of light emphasizing particular areas of a room or collections of precious objects of art, for instance.

4

STRATEGY

A *BEAUTIFUL HOME,* elegantly coloured, attractively finished, well lighted, functional and warm, is everyone's dream. But the steps from *here* to *there* can mean massive disruption in day-to-day life, as well as considerable expense. The first priority when thinking out what action needs to be taken in a new home is to avoid wasting money on inappropriate or downright foolish schemes. Never forget that any form of home improvement, particularly if it involves the renovation of an entire house or apartment, will also involve considerable stress on you and the rest of the household.

Home renovation has emotional consequences which few people new to this area of life consider in the beginning. Now is the moment when you may have to realize that your taste and that of your partner may not exactly coincide. If that is the case (and it often is, in matters of taste and style) your first step will be to negotiate with each other about what the end result is supposed to be. This must please you both for years to come and not leave one person resentful of aesthetic choices, the amount of work contributed and, of course, the vital question of financial responsibility. Learning to communicate design ideas, to trust and support each other as they are put into execution is a way of strengthening relationships, but if work is not planned properly from the outset, it can have a destructive effect. Understanding the stages of work and strategically advancing them from inception to finished success should be the aim in both emotional and practical terms.

First steps

Before starting to plan your new colour schemes, first consider any building or architectural problems which need immediate attention. Good repairs, up-dating and maintenance also affect the re-sale value of your property, so, in your imagination, strip your home down to its bare bones and look at the following points:

■ Is the property really dry? A sound roof, gutters, downpipes and an effective damp-proof course are the enduring basis for all future work.

■ Is the electrical wiring sufficiently up-to-date? Re-wiring is a messy business, often involving the raking out of plaster channels in the walls and the lifting of floor boards. Good, modern wiring is as essential to safety as to good re-sale value and, when planning electrical receptacles (sockets), it is always best to err on the side of too many rather than too few, never forgetting awkward areas like landings where they are essential for stair cleaning.

■ What state is the joinery in? In damp climates, slowly decaying wooden window and door frames are an on-going hazard. Well-fitting, water-tight exterior joinery greatly enhances the re-sale value of a home but, in an older property, do not be tempted into a quick-fix solution of new aluminium frames or any "out of period" joinery which may spoil the character of the building or street. Nowadays, architectural good manners in conserving details can certainly reap financial rewards. Conservation studies have shown that overtly and crudely modernized properties have lower re-sale value than those where the style of the original building has been respected and maintained.

■ Even if your taste is modern, dramatic and clean-cut, it is best not to remove any original features such as good, decorative plasterwork, stained glass, mouldings, panelled doors, shutters and well-turned banisters. If you find their cumulative effect too fussy, this can be remedied by colour and furnishing, but potential buyers prefer to see them retained *in situ*. If, for example, you really must remove old doors and their surrounds because they are part of a wall which is to be demolished, have them removed carefully and store them to offer to a new potential buyer. The same is true of stained glass, old tiling and fireplaces.

■ The kitchen is the room which will demand most money because of the joinery, tiling, lighting and installations we would all, ideally, like to see there. For people on a budget, the kitchen is the room which is most often developed in two stages over a number of years. Spend money getting the structure right first and then, when finance permits, begin to fill it in with those coveted fixtures and fittings.

HIRING A BUILDER

When tackling a job which involves, say, knocking holes in a load-bearing wall, or levelling a floor to lay a screed, you may need to hire a local builder. The best way to find a builder is still by word-of-mouth recommendation, after which you can go along discreetly to see the finished job, enquire about costs (whether they ran wildly over budget, for example), time-keeping and general attitude to the work. One sign of any good craftsperson is that he or she always cleans up neatly at the end of a session and does not leave you to wade through unnecessary debris.

Professional building organizations often keep lists of builders who specialize in certain types of work, such as extensions. Should finding a builder by word-of-mouth prove difficult, these organizations usually recommend that you always employ someone who is registered with a recognized trade body. Then, if something goes seriously wrong, you will have recourse to official arbitration.

If possible, try to find three builders to quote for work as prices can vary wildly, even for comparatively small jobs. You should set aside at least a month to get in quotes from builders for the job you want done. To obtain a realistic quote, you must communicate your aims clearly: a detailed sketch plan is better than standing waving your arms about. From each builder you should eventually receive in writing one of two things:

■ **An estimate** – a guide to the price that will be charged when the job is finished; this may turn out to be slightly more or less than the price stated.

■ **A quotation** – a fixed price for which the builder will agree to do the job. He might, however, put in a contingency sum for unforeseen problems that may arise.

For large, complicated jobs, such as the renovation of a whole house, ask the builder to draw up a **schedule list**. This sets out clearly each stage of the work, e.g. building a blockwork wall, plastering, supplying and fitting a bath and basin etc. Sometimes items such as baths, sinks etc. may be marked with words "prime cost". This is usually an approximate price set aside to cover the cost of such a fitting when you actually go to a showroom to choose it.

Start and finish dates should also be discussed with the builder. You can ask for a **time schedule** here, but a reasonable degree of flexibility should be expected. Find out how much of the work is to be sub-contracted to electricians, plumbers and joiners. If much of the work is to be sub-contracted, delays are more likely to occur.

ORDER OF WORK

■ Decide on the overall scheme and measure each room carefully. If the work involves any structural alterations, draw a simple sketch plan of what you want done. Plan lighting effects carefully and mark receptacle (socket) positions on your plan.

■ Decide how much of the work you can do yourself and how much you intend to put out to a builder, carpenter, plumber, electrician or other skilled professional.

■ If you are tackling a whole house, it is usual to begin with the functional areas such as kitchen and bathroom and then work down from the top of the house leaving the staircase and

hall until last. If you are going to have to live in the property while work is going on, begin to organize your "bunker". Set aside one room in which you cam make yourself comfortable, with a bed, television, music, electric kettle, microwave and easy access to clothes. This will be your retreat from which you shut the door on the general disturbance for weeks to come.

■ Strip the house or apartment of furniture, pictures, china and fittings. If you have so much furniture that you need to arrange for its storage, get quotes for storage from several removal companies. Otherwise, stack all the furniture in one room and cover it with cheap drop cloths or dust sheets. In rooms with large items such as a piano or big cupboard, pull the piece into the centre of the room and cover it. Lift and roll up linoleum and carpets.

■ The builder can then proceed with the structural works.

If you are hiring builders for basic structural work make sure you brief them in which original woodwork and fixtures you would like to preserve before they start work.

■ Shortly before the building work is completed, set aside time for "snagging". This means checking that all work has been done to your satisfaction i.e., that all loose floor boards have been secured, that all windows and doors open and close properly, that all services such as water, gas, electricity and central heating have been reconnected and are running efficiently.

■ Have the chimney swept if necessary.

■ Check on tools and hire any specialist ones that you may need for preparation and decoration. (See information on equipment hire below).

■ Preparation can now begin in the sequence given in Chapter 7, followed by decoration of the rooms.

Equipment Hire

The tools and equipment you will have to buy for both preparation and decorative work are given in Chapters 5, 6 and 7. When budgeting for an entire home renovation and decorative scheme, you must also cost in the fact that, in the early stages, you will probably have to hire one or more large pieces of heavy-duty equipment. Hiring some tools may seem rather expensive at the time, particularly if you only use them for a couple of hours, but nothing speeds up a job like an appropriate specialist tool, and in many ways it can make up for an initial lack of expertise.

It is always worth ringing around tool-hire shops to compare prices. Small firms often charge less but they may have a more limited range available, fewer up-to-date models and many of the tools they offer may be a bit on the battered side. More upmarket outlets which may be part of a large chain offer a free colour catalogue of all the tools and equipment they stock, provide full operating instructions with every tool and the chance to order over the telephone by credit card for quick delivery. Wherever you hire tools from, you are entitled to ask for an operating demonstration.

SCAFFOLDING AND SUPPORT PLATFORMS

Scaffolding and support platforms are invaluable for decorating jobs, particularly in awkward areas such as stairwells. Decorator's trestles are available in alloy and wood and are used with lightweight staging to provide a stable working platform. Nowadays, such scaffolding and support platforms are often the snap-together types which are simple to erect at home. Large hire shops can also offer folding step-up platforms which can fit into a car, as well as ingenious folding ladders which can be hinged to stand safely in any direction.

Other equipment you may want to hire includes

■ **A wallpaper stripper** (see p.90);

■ **A hot air paint stripper** (see p.98);

■ **A hand-operated tile cutter** (a very useful tool to hire if you are intending to tile floor or wall areas yourself. It is a box-like tool with a carbide wheel mounted in it for the easy cutting to size of ceramic or quarry floor and wall tiles up to ⅝in [15mm] thick. When hiring any tile-cutting tool, it is always best to take along a sample of the tiles you will be using);

■ **A floor-sander** (this should be used in conjunction with an **edging sander**, which lets you strip the wood right up to the baseboards [skirting boards]. Although sanders have dust collection bags, the outflow of dust will be still very high and you should attempt to seal off the room before you begin working. Make absolutely certain that you always wear a dustmask when sanding. Buy a generous quantity of abrasive sheets to use on the sander in coarse, medium and fine grades. Check that the shop will buy back any sheets you do not use).

When working with powerful tools, always keep safety uppermost in your mind. Most high-quality hire shops will also supply safety equipment such as goggles, dust or spray masks, ear defenders, protective gloves and disposable overalls. *Always* wear these – better safe than sorry.

5

DECORATIVE EQUIPMENT

HAVING THE RIGHT tool for the job is as important for decorating as any other form of do-it-yourself home improvements. For some types of decorative work you must have the correct equipment, however sometimes it is possible to improvise. There is a plethora of gadgets available nowadays, some of these may make the job easier, others will just waste your money.

Traditional decorator's equipment is really the best thing to spend your money on. More and more gadgets claiming to make the job easier seem to appear daily. It is possible these things do make life easier for the rank amateur but it is always quicker if you use the proper tools, and they will help to do a better job. A little hands-on experience is all that is needed; after all, if these gadgets were so good all the professionals would be using them.

The best place to purchase your equipment is in a trade shop. Trade shops always have an excellent range of products at a competitive price. For paint, paint merchants will supply most of the equipment needed for decorative effects and they will of course have the every-day paints and paint thinner (white spirit), and will usually stock transparent oil glazes, acrylic scumbles and varnishes and some specialist brushes. The decorative painter's suppliers will stock all the specialist products and the type of products usually found in art shops such as artist's brushes and oil and acrylic colours.

Brushes, gadgets and tools

The minimum number of brushes required is a couple of 1 in (25 mm) and 2 in (50 mm) brushes and a 4 in (100 mm), plus a 6 in (150 mm) latex (emulsion) brush (if you do not have a roller and tray). Buy the best you can afford; cheap brushes do not last and give a poorer finish. Also, the bristles tend to fall out spoiling your paintwork. These different-size brushes are essential for preparation and are also quite adequate for applying glazes as well as varnishing and applying specialist products such as water-based furniture paint and water-based acrylic primer. These brushes can also be used for dragging, the 6 in (150 mm) brush being very handy for dragging walls.

Special brushes tend to be expensive so only buy those you rally need. Fitches are long-handled brushes with firm bristles useful for spattering and stippling small areas, also good for painting areas you cannot quite reach from a stepladder. A "softening" bristle brush is necessary for blending glazes and is essential for marbling. A decorator's dusting brush is a cheap alternative and can also be used for stippling small areas. Badger-hair softeners are very expensive; they are only really needed for professional work. Gliders are very useful for applying glazes and varnishing and are available in a wide variety of sizes. Stippling brushes are the fastest and only practical way of stippling walls, and a smaller brush could only be used on a small wall area or on furniture. Unfortunately these brushes are very expensive. A flogger is essential for woodgraining and can also be used for dragging. Over-grainers are used for adding detail when wood-graining and come in a variety of types. For stencilling you can use a stencilling brush with bristles trimmed flat for stippling colours or a more rounded brush if you prefer to brush the colour on. Artist's brushes are invaluable for detailed decorative work and for touching up damaged paintwork. A lining brush is like an artist's brush with very long bristles; it holds more colour so is good for painting longer lines without stopping.

A wooden truckle is always useful for keeping essential equipment near at hand.

OTHER TOOLS AND EQUIPMENT

You will probably need certain basic items:

Scrapers You will need these broad-headed tools to remove old wallpaper. A triangular scraper or shavehook is used to remove old paint from mouldings and complex surfaces.

Sandpaper Never underestimate how much sandpaper you will get through. It comes in various grades from very coarse (for the initial rubbing down) to very fine (for the final finish). A cork block round which to wrap the paper and so gain greater "purchase" against the surface is also useful. Silicon carbide (wet and dry) paper is used for sanding between coats of paints and for keying surfaces before painting.

Plastic bucket Used for mixing up wallpaper paste and for washing down surfaces.

A sponge Useful for washing down surfaces. Use a natural sponge for sponging paint on and off, and a synthetic sponge for applying colourwash.

Papering table Essential for pasting liner (lining) paper and wallpaper and costs surprisingly little.

Scissors Long-bladed scissors for cutting paper will probably be fairly expensive but are worth buying. Do not use good household scissors for this job as paper blunts them.

Tape measure Needed for measuring lengths of paper.

Stepladder Every home needs a stepladder and decorating cannot be done without one. Aluminium ladders are best as they are light to carry and one with a platform is essential for holding cans of paint and tools.

Drop cloths or dustsheets Thin, cheap polythene dustsheets are only useful for protecting furniture from dust and paint spots. Heavy cotton drop cloths or dustsheets are best for protecting the floor. They are also non-slip and protect a newly sanded floor from dents as well as from dust and spatters of paint and other materials.

Papering brush and seam roller These are essential for ensuring that paper stays firmly on the wall after positioning.

Brushes and applicators

Having the right brush for the job is extremely important. It is worth spending money on a good collection of high-quality brushes, taking care to clean them thoroughly after use and storing them appropriately. For the specialist brush ranges hair comes from a variety of animals, such as sable, ox, badger and squirrel. Hog hair or horse hair are tougher and these brushes are normally used for oil and latex (emulsion) work.

7 Goose feather, for marbling

8 Sable water colour brushes of varying sizes; essential for painting small areas

9 Coach liner, used for lining

10 Sword liner, for lining

11 Soft mop head brush, good for dusting metal powders and powder pigments

6 Metal combs for wood-graining and strong combed effects

1 & 2 1 in (25 mm) and 2 in (50 mm) glider's varnish brushes; can also be used for dragging

3 4 in (100 mm) hog hair softener for colourwashing and softening scumble effect. Can also be used for stippling

5 Hog hair stencilling brush

4 Horse hair flogger for woodgraining. The stiff horse hair bristles leave the splintering look of woodgrain when banged flat against the wet glaze

20 Rubber rocker, pulled down through a wet glaze to imitate woodgrain

⑬

13 Natural sponge, for sponged glaze effects

㉑

21 Round end stencil brushes, excellent for shading colours

㉒

22 Wire brush, for rubbing down old metal before painting

⑳

⑫

12 Synthetic household sponge, for colourwashing or making stamps

⑱

18 Fitches, useful for mixing colours

⑮

⑭

⑯

⑰

⑲

14 & 15 ½ in (12 mm) and 1 in (25 mm) flat end brushes, used for painting small objects or areas with intricate mouldings

16 Badger-hair softener – the finest and most expensive softener for oil glaze work such as marblizing and woodgraining

17 Birch twigs, for spatter techniques

19 1½ (40 mm) decorator's brush, for general use

PURE BADGER
MADE IN ENGLAND

■ **Paint brushes** A good range of paint brushes is essential –
perhaps a couple of 1 in (25 mm), a 2 in (50 mm) and a 4 in
(100 mm) for the woodwork and a 6 in (150 mm) latex
(emulsion) brush for the walls. A roller with a removable sleeve
and a roller tray is useful if you are in a hurry.

■ **Paint kettle** This is a cheap, plastic container useful for
decanting paint from a big can. It is also useful for washing out
brushes once you have finished.

A pale green colourwashed
effect created with strong,
haphazard brush strokes
produced by a wide softening
brush.

■ **Rags** These are always handy for cleaning colour samples off walls and spills off the floor. They are also used for ragging. Try not to use rags which shed fibres as these will spoil finished surfaces. Mutton cloth is an alternative to home-made rags; it can be bought from decorator's shops.

■ **Craft knife** A knife with replaceable blades is necessary for cutting stencils as well as a multitude of other tasks.

■ **Hairdrier** Useful for drying off paint samples quickly to see what the colours look like when dry.

■ **Flood light** Powerful lighting is always useful in the winter or in darker areas: good light and hence good visibility are very important for all types of painting.

USEFUL HOUSEHOLD EQUIPMENT TO COLLECT

Glass jars with lids are always worth keeping to store any left-over glaze after finishing a room so that you have a supply of the correct colour for touching up any damaged areas. Left-over paint can also be stored in jars. Remember to label anything stored in a container. Cardboard boxes are a convenient way of storing all the smaller bits and pieces of decorating equipment that always seem to accumulate. Remember to keep any old sheets for rags.

As kitchen storage jars are completely airtight, they make excellent receptacles for preserving powder pigments or paint.

STORAGE AND MAINTENANCE

You will need a surprising amount of space to store all your equipment and also all those half-empty cans of paint. The best place is a clean and dry garage or shed, especially if you intend to keep oil-based paints which cannot be stored in the house because of their flammability. Brushes need the most care in storage; they should always be washed out thoroughly after use and can be stored hanging from nails if you drill holes in the handles, or if space is at a premium keep them upside down in a paint kettle when they are dry. The main thing is to make sure the bristles are not damaged, especially important in the case of delicate and expensive specialist brushes.

Tools and equipment

There are some essential tools needed for preparation as well as general decorating jobs which are definitely worth buying. It is wise to keep them in good condition and to store them carefully, away from children, when not in use. Wear gloves to protect your hands when using them.

1 Ceramic tile, available from any home improvement or bathroom store; tiles are very useful for mixing paints, particularly water-based ones

2 Ceramic dish, useful for mixing paste or particularly runny solutions

5 Plumb line, essential for creating straight lines in a decorative scheme. It comprises a cord weighted at the bottom, which is coated in chalk and then pressed against the wall to leave a faint impression

3 Wire brush, ideal for roughening old paint surfaces for stripping or creating distressed effects on new paint-work

4 Glass jar, particularly useful for storing samples of any paints used so that accurate matching at a later date is possible if re-touching is required

6 Paint opener: some paint suppliers stock specially designed openers which are perfect for levering up new and old lids

9 Triangular scraper or shavehook: this combines curved and straight edges, and is excellent for stripping paintwork from curved objects or mouldings

11 Sandpaper comes in different grades including coarse, medium and fine. Silicon carbide (wet-and-dry) paper is used with water to prevent the paper from becoming clogged with fine particles

10 Tape measure: a long, retractable tape measure is always useful

12 Sanding block, has the sandpaper wrapped around it and acts as a support

7 & 8 Spatulas have many mixing, scraping and filling uses. Also used for stripping small areas of old paint or wallpaper on a small scale

13 & 14 Wire wool is available in different grades, and is used to rub down surfaces to a very smooth finish, to distress new paintwork and for rubbing waxes into various surfaces

Decorating equipment

M any decorative paint techniques involve the use of equipment commonly found in the kitchen, bathroom or tool shed. It is useful to collect these and provides a way of recycling different objects and materials. It is worth investigating trade suppliers of catering equipment for bulk supplies of useful utensils such as plastic spoons for decanting and paper plates for easy colour mixing.

2 Mini roller, used for applying even coats of paint to rubber stamps or creating fine stripes; also for decorating areas of a room that are difficult to reach

1 Candle wax can provide a barrier between materials, stopping one from adhering to another. This is useful for water-based distressing techniques

3 Rubber stamps, used for applying repeated decorative motifs to walls, furniture or fabric

4 Cotton buds, useful for cleaning fine mouldings or decorative carvings, or for blotting hand-painted decoration

8 Chalk, for tracing in designs before applying colour

5 Corks are perfect for carving stamp designs into, for example in some traditional Scandinavian decorative techniques e.g. basket painting

6 Embroidery scissors, essential for delicate crafts that involve precise or intricate cutting e.g. découpage

7 Craft knife, essential for cutting stencils, cork stamps and découpage motifs

9 Cotton rag: cotton sheeting is the best fabric for ragging and rag rolling effects which leave an imprint of the fabric in a wet scumble glaze

10 Chamois leather, used in ragging effects; the leather absorbs wet glaze to a greater extent than cotton rag the imprints left are sharper

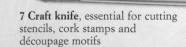

15 Plastic spoons, useful for mixing and decanting different materials (remember that paint thinner [white spirit] based solutions will eventually) dissolve the plastic

13 Transfer paper is a thin tissue-like paper with a coloured chalk film on one side

18 Modelling putty, useful for pressing into wet glazes to create abstract shapes

14 Tracing paper, used for tracing designs in pencil onto various surfaces, it can also be used for covering small amounts of oil pigment to prevent them forming a crust

11 Stencil card is an oiled card used for creating motifs

12 Transparent plastic film, used to cut stencils. This is very flexible and good for bending around corners

19 Flexible curve, very useful for drawing smooth curves by hand

16 Low-tack masking tape, used for sticking things temporarily, for masking off areas when creating a design, or for creating straight lines

17 Lining tape, a thin, red plastic tape used for creating fine lines on furniture

20 Plastic wrap (cling film) can also be pressed into wet glazes to leave a delicate, rippling effect

6

PAINTS AND FINISHES

PAINT IS EXTRAORDINARY stuff. Just think about it. A layer of material less than 1/16 in (1 mm) thick protects a surface from deterioration and also adds colour and texture, and can even create an illusion. It has to be tough enough to take knocks and bashes and to withstand chemical attack. Of course no single paint can possess all the properties required for a particular site and different paints are used for different jobs. The purpose of this chapter is to give you an insight into what paint consists of and its different types, how paint was made in the past and what goes into it today.

Paint basically consists of three main ingredients, a filler to give the paint bulk and covering power, a pigment to give it colour and a binder to hold it all together. These are always either suspended or dissolved in a liquid medium which enables you to brush it onto a surface. The liquid evaporates allowing the main ingredient to bond together chemically thereby providing a coloured, protective surface. The liquid medium used is either water or an oil and the make-up and properties of these two types of paint are quite different. (Of course, today it is far more complicated than this in practice; there are many more ingredients than those mentioned above and also there are highly specialized paints which are outside the scope of this book, as it is mainly concerned with decorative paints.)

The origins of paint

Paints have always been based on either water or oil. Traditionally oil-based paints were tougher than water-based paints and were used on woodwork, whereas water-based paints were used on walls. Artists have always used both types of paint for paintings. Early oil paintings were made from linseed oil (derived from the seeds of the flax plant), drying agents which accelerated the drying rate, and pigment for colouring. The solvent used was turpentine, which is derived from the resin of the terebinth tree. White lead was used as a filler and whitener for hundreds of years and makes a durable paint that ages very gracefully. Nowadays titanium dioxide has replaced the poisonous lead and is also used in water-based paint. Historically, water-based paints were very simple and it is easy to make them at home. Limewash is one example: water and lime are mixed together and pigment is added before the mixture is brushed onto the wall. The lime acts as both whitener and binder and the resulting finish is very soft and chalky looking. The finish allows the wall to breathe rather than forming an impermeable layer and also has the added advantage as acting as a disinfectant.

Fitches are ideal for experimenting with and mixing paint colours, whether oil- or water-based.

Another simple wall finish that was widely used was distemper; in this whiting, or specially prepared chalk, acts as a whitener and filler and is bound by a rabbit-skin glue with pigment added. This also gives a very soft and chalky finish; oil can be added to give the distemper durability.

The range of pigments available before the eighteenth century was rather limited; most colours were derived from the earth pigments such as the siennas and umbers, sometimes from plants and powdered minerals such as lapis lazuli. Chemists in the eighteenth century discovered a wider range of cheaper colours, and nowadays colours are made from aniline dyes, synthetic pigments derived from coal-tar.

MODERN PAINTS AND NEW DEVELOPMENTS IN PAINT TECHNOLOGY

Modern paints have rather different properties from their historical forbears. Oil-based paints are now made from alkyd resins and have similar properties to the older oil paints in that they have always been very durable. Modern water-based paints are much more permanent and much tougher than limewashes and distempers, and many are now washable. Water-based paints are based on plastics such as polyvinyl acetate which form a plastic film over a surface and seal in the wall.

In recent years concern has been expressed over the long-term health effects of the solvents used in oil-based paints and their contribution to atmospheric pollution. Alternatives have been developed from acrylic polymers, a tougher plastic than polyvinyl acetate. These new paints are water-based and have none of the obvious drawbacks of the oil-based paints. It is now possible to buy direct replacements of the traditional oil-based paints in acrylic form; they are usually prefixed by the term "acrylic" or "quick-drying", as in "acrylic scumble glaze" or "quick-drying" oil or gloss paint, traditionally an oil-based paint. These new paints are as tough as their oil-based counterparts but dry more quickly. However they do have a different, somewhat plastic quality and their speed in drying can sometimes be a problem, for example when a broken colour effect is needed. In these cases retardants (such as glycerine or acrylic scrumble glaze) can be added to slow down the drying time of the water-based alternatives.

Recent developments in the paint world have brought us water-based acrylic scumble glazes for techniques such as dragging (top) and high-build textured paints to create rustic wall finishes (bottom).

Raw materials and solvents

It is useful to know what the basic ingredients of paints are, especially for those who want to try their hand at mixing some home-made versions. Historic paints certainly have qualities that are difficult to imitate with synthetic, contemporary materials, and may be just what you need if you have original paint finishes to restore. It is useful to keep a small stock at least of powder pigments which have multiple uses from tinting paint to dusting on dry as an antiquing device.

1 Paint thinner (white spirit), a cheaper form of turpentine which is the solvent for all oil-based mediums

2 Denatured alcohol (methylated spirit), stained purple in the UK to indicate its harmful quality but colourless in the States, this is an alcohol-based solvent for shellacs and spirit-based varnishes

3 Water, the solvent for latex (emulsion) paints and all acrylic-based products

POWDER PIGMENTS

4-13 Naturally produced earth, mineral or vegetable powders that have provided the tints for colouring paint since prehistoric times. Sold in small quantities, these are pure and very expensive.

4 Ultramarine

9 Green earth

5 Ultraviolet

10 Yellow ochre

11 Slate grey

6 Manganese black

12 Venetian red

8 Cobalt blue

13 Burnt umber

7 Cerulean blue

15 Rabbit-skin glue, obtained from the skin of rabbits, this is available in granule or sheet form and is used as a binder in gesso

14 PVA (Polyvinyl acrylic), a versatile water-based material which can be used as a tough glue, sealant or binder

16 Whiting, a natural calcium carbonate ground to a fine powder. This is an ingredient in gesso and traditional paints such as distemper

17 Gum arabic, a naturally produced, water-soluble gum in liquid or crystal form. It is used as a medium for water colour and gouache paints as well as forming delicate glue

19 Acrylic scumble glaze, a water-based scumble glaze made from acrylic resins which is tinted with acrylic paints and used for dragging, ragging, stippling and sponging

20 Oil-based scumble glaze is made from linseed oil, driers and resins and is diluted with paint thinner (white spirit)

18 Linseed oil, a basic ingredient of traditional oil paints, and is obtained from the seeds of the flax plant

22 Metallic powders, made from copper, silver, aluminium or alloys. They need to be protected from oxidation with coats of varnish or shellac

21 Universal stainer, a concentrated colouring agent or dye that can be used to tint either oil- or water-based substances

Water-based paints

The advantages of water-based paints are that they are quick-drying, have no unpleasant odour and any equipment used can be washed easily in warm, soapy water. Traditionally used for walls, in the past these paints, such as distemper, were mixed using animal glues as a binder, which, being organic, eventually decayed if left for more than a few days in their wet form. Despite this some people still prefer to mix these traditional paints using the original materials as they do have a wonderfully chalky and very rich finish. However, the most commonly used water-based paints today are those known as flat (matt) or vinyl latex paints or emulsions. Made up of synthetic polymer acetates or acrylic polymers, these paints do tend to be less porous, as the surface is coated in a film; this means they can be washed down repeatedly.

Produced commercially in most countries these water-based paints are the cheapest and most easily obtainable. Available in flat (matt), satin or mid-sheen (eggshell), or gloss finishes they can be hand-tinted using powder pigments, acrylic colours or universal stainers, although most reputable paint companies now offer a quick and efficient colour mixing service.

Apart from providing opaque coats for walls these paints can be used as a base for decorative effects such as colour-washing, glaze finishes or stencilling. They can be diluted to create washes of colour though it is advisable to use some form of retardant, such as acrylic scumble glaze, to slow down the drying process and so aid the application. These paints could also be used for hand painting (though they would need two coats of varnish), and can be applied directly to new plaster as well as to porous surfaces such as brickwork or breeze blocks.

For a period feel some designers are returning to flat, chalky finishes provided by the new superior quality latex (emulsion) paints that many historic ranges now offer.

Water-based materials

TYPE	CONSTITUTION	PROPERTIES	USES
PAINT MAGIC IMPASTO PAINT (*textured paint*)	Acrylic emulsion polymer, chalk, cellulose ether	Very thick white product. Will cover anything, and can be sanded smooth.	Used on walls to give an attractive textured finish. Designed to be colourwashed subsequently to produce a rustic finish.
PAINT MAGIC COLOURWASH (*colourwash paint*)	Polyvinyl acetate (PVA) pigment, drying retardant	Gives a soft, matt "fresco" look. Partially transparent. Easy to use, quick drying. Can be wiped clean.	Used as a convenient and quick-to-apply wall finish.
PAINT MAGIC WOODWASH, (*flat latex [matt emulsion] paint*)	PVA, high degree of pigmentation	Matt finish that can be buffed to a sheen. Very opaque although can be diluted with water to give a semi-transparent finish. Hard-wearing, fully washable.	A very convenient furniture paint as no primer or undercoats required. Used neat, covers wood in one coat otherwise dilute with water to allow the woodgrain to show through.
FLAT OR SATIN LATEX (MATT OR VINYL SILK EMULSION) PAINT	PVA, pigments. Silk emulsion has more PVA and less pigmentation	Matt version very opaque. Absorbent. Can be used on new plaster. Quick drying and washable. Silk emulsion less opaque but tougher and virtually non-absorbent. Cannot be used on new plaster. Darker colours can look very heavy.	Cheap, readily available wall paint that comes in a huge range of colours. Can be diluted with water and used as a colourwash if you are very fast with the paint brush.

TYPE	CONSTITUTION	PROPERTIES	USES
ACRYLIC SATIN (EGGSHELL) PAINT	Acrylic polymers, pigment	Satin finish. Opaque and non-absorbent. Hard-wearing and fully washable. Quick drying, tendency for brush marks to show; not available in very dark colours.	Versatile paint for use on woodwork and walls, used as a base for acrylic scumble glaze. Can use oil scumbles over it if allowed a few days to dry.
ACRYLIC GLOSS	Acrylic polymers, pigment	Gloss finish. Not as opaque as the satin (eggshell) finish. Non-absorbent. Very hard-wearing and fully washable. Quick drying; tendency for brush marks to show, not as glossy as the oil-based version.	Used as an alternative to oil-based gloss for interior and exterior woodwork.
ACRYLIC WOOD PRIMER/ UNDERCOAT	Acrylic polymers, high degree of white pigment	Matt finish that is very opaque. High build properties, designed to be overpainted.	Covers bare wood very well eliminating the need for an undercoat. Can be used as a cheap alternative to acrylic gesso.
PAINT MAGIC ACRYLIC CONVERTOR (*acrylic primer*)	Acrylic polymers	A primer which is designed to adhere to oil-based paints.	Enables you to overpaint oil-based paint with water-based paint, traditionally a problem area.
ACRYLIC SCUMBLE GLAZE	Acrylic polymers, drying retardant	Transparent medium designed to have colour added to it and to retain an imprint on the wet surface.	Used for decorative techniques such as ragging, stippling, sponging, marbling and woodgraining.

Oil-based paints

Oil-based paints are tougher and more durable than water-based paints. They are particularly suitable for protecting the surfaces in a room such as the doors and baseboards (skirting) which will experience a greater degree of wear and tear. Oil-based paints will also provide a waterproof coat.

However, the solvent used in oil-based paints is paint thinner (white spirit). This means that the paints are toxic and have an unpleasant smell, so take care to always work in a well-ventilated area when using them. Oil-based paints dry more slowly than water-based paints which can be advantageous when applying certain paint effects.

Although there are now water-based equivalents for virtually all oil-based mediums, some professionals still prefer to stick to oil-based paints when creating scumble glaze effects, particularly when working on a large scale. This is because the oil-based medium dries very slowly and the glaze remains wet or "open" for much longer, allowing more time for the manipulation of an effect such as stippling or ragging. Other instances where an oil-based paint is preferable is if a gloss finish is desired – the finish is much smoother than the water-based equivalent – and also when priming metal surfaces which can rust if coated in a water-based medium.

TYPE	CONSTITUTION	PROPERTIES	USES
MID-SHEEN SATIN (EGGSHELL) PAINT	Synthetic alkyd resin, driers, pigments	Satin finish. Opaque and non-absorbent. Hard-wearing and fully washable. Slow drying. Gives a fine, smooth surface.	Popular as a woodwork finish. An excellent base for oil-based scumble glaze. Consider using water-based alternatives on walls because of the strong fumes.
GLOSS	Oil-modified alkyd resin, pigment	High gloss finish that is very hard-wearing and fully washable. Slow drying, gives a rich, deep shine.	Used on woodwork, particularly where a high degree of protection is required, such as on exterior surfaces.
SCUMBLE GLAZE	Linseed oil, driers and resins	Transparent medium that is designed to have colour added to it. Takes and retains an imprint. Slow drying. Washable. Will yellow, particularly in the absence of light.	Used for decorative techniques such as ragging, dragging, stippling, marbling and woodgraining. Normally used diluted with paint thinner (white spirit).

Artist's paints

This group refers to those paints used for fine art, murals and decorative furniture painting and tinting. The pigments used are very concentrated so are more expensive and come in smaller quantities than decorating paints. The colour ranges are not standardized so you may find that there are variations in the same colours offered by different companies. There are also cheaper, "student" ranges available where the pigments used are not as refined although there is little difference in the final appearance.

Artist's paints can be oil- or water-based. Water colours, which come in either a tube or as a dry block, can be used for creating soft, transparent washes of colour. However, because of their delicacy they are really only suitable for painting on paper or card. For furniture painting, gouache paints could be used, these are more intense in colour and are bound with chalk to make them more opaque than water colours. Acrylic artist's colours are probably the toughest because of their synthetic medium and they dry very quickly allowing further layers or shading to be applied. They can also be used for stencilling, stamping or printing on walls, furniture or fabric.

Artist's oil colours are very rich, dense and of course they dry very slowly (some oil paintings can take months to dry) though this can be a great advantage for techniques such as craquelure, where oil colour is rubbed into the fine cracks and then gently buffed off while still wet. Both water- and oil-based artist's colours can be diluted with their respective solvents to create antiquing washes for ageing new paintwork. The earth colours such as raw umber or burnt sienna are particularly good colours for this purpose.

TYPE	CONSTITUTION	PROPERTIES	USES
DRY POWDER PIGMENTS	Mineral or synthetic dry powder	Available in a wide range of colours and qualities, the best ones are very finely ground.	Used to add colour to paint. As they are dry they can be added to any type of paint. Can be more economical to use than artist's colours.
OIL COLOURS	Linseed oil and pigment	Concentrated colour that is supplied in various-size tubes. Two qualities available: student's and artist's. Artist's oils are more concentrated with finely ground pigments. Soluble in paint thinner. Slow drying.	Used by artists for oil painting. The most convenient way of tinting oil-based paints and glazes. Wide range of colours available that can be intermixed to provide almost limitless colour possibilities.
ACRYLIC COLOURS	Acrylic medium and pigment	Available in tubes and plastic bottles. Similar colour range to oil colours. Water soluble and fast drying. Quite tough when dry. Very opaque unless thinned with water or clear acrylic medium.	Useful for mural painting and tinting water-based paints and glazes. Very convenient for stencilling and applied decoration because of the quick drying time.
WATER COLOURS	Gum arabic and pigment	Available in tiny tubes and solid blocks. Clear transparent colours. Water soluble.	Mainly used by artists diluted with water for water colour painting.

Paint types

When choosing a paint for a particular job it is important to appreciate how the types differ enormously in their consistency, properties and final finish. In some cases there are only a few that will be suitable for doing the job successfully so do your homework thoroughly.

2 Water colour, for delicate washes on paper

3 Gouache, water colour mixed with chalk to make it opaque; used for delicate decoration

1 Spray paint contained in an aerosol can be used for stencilling large-scale effects and applying colour to pieces which are difficult to paint with a brush

4 Acrylic paint, multi-purpose; can be used to add a tint, as a wash or in opaque form for fine art or furniture painting

5 Oil paint, used for centuries by fine artists; can be used diluted or in impasto techniques. It dries very slowly and is extremely rich, so is useful for adding strong tints

ARTIST'S COLOURS

TRADITIONAL PAINTS

LATEX AND OIL-BASED PAINTS

6 **Distemper**, made from whiting, rabbit-skin glue and pigment 7 **Limewash**, made from slaked lime 8 **Casein** paint, derived from non-fat milk solids 9 **Impasto paint**, a modern textured paint

METALLIC AND LACQUEUR PAINTS

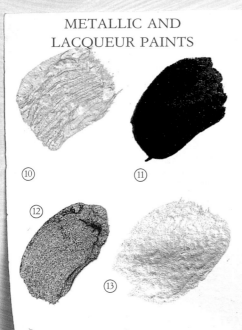

Gloss finishes: **14 Oil-based gloss 15 Water-based gloss**. Mid-sheen finishes: **16 Oil-based** (also known as eggshell) **17 Water-based**, known as vinyl silk. Flat (matt) finishes: **18 Oil-based flat 19 Water-based flat latex (matt emulsion)**

SPECIALIZED WATER-BASED PAINTS

10 **Silver**, oil-based enamel paint 11 **Bronze**, spirit-based metallic paint 12 **Acrylic gold stencil paint** 13 **Oil-based Japan paint**, a high-gloss black finish paint

20 **Proprietary colourwash**, a ready-mixed, transparent, water-based glaze for walls with a retardant in it that keeps it "open" for manipulation 21 **Woodwash**, a thick, rich furniture paint that can be burnished with wire wool or polished with waxes

Waxes, Varnishes and Stains

Waxes can be used to protect new woodwork as well as to give a rich, mellow patina to existing paintwork. Different sources produce different coloured waxes – such as pale yellow beeswax from honeycombs, white Japan wax from berries, dark brown carnauba wax from a Brazilian palm – and successive layers will buff up gently with age. Waxes can be softened with heat and powder pigments added to create an antiquing paste for mouldings and carved features. Wax also plays an important part in heavy distressing techniques where it is sandwiched between two different coloured paints as a resisting barrier. When rubbed back with wire wool, the top coat will come away where the wax was applied to reveal the colour underneath.

Like waxes, stains also provide protection for woodwork. Applied directly to new, untreated wood, they penetrate and preserve the grain, at the same time adding transparent colour. Water-based stains are less durable than oil- or spirit-based ones and must be varnished afterwards. Oil-based stains tend to penetrate deeply and feed the grain, while spirit-based ones offer a wider range of colours but are thinner and dry quickly. Some stains are tinted to imitate a particular type of wood while others are a stain and varnish combined.

It is easy to confuse varnishes and lacquers though in fact there are great differences. Historically, varnishes were developed from the resins and gums from particular trees which, when added to natural oils, were insoluble in water and dried to create a hard, glossy, protective coating. Today synthetic resins are used and matting agents added to provide different degrees of gloss. As oil-based varnishes tend to yellow with time and contain paint thinner (white spirit) as a solvent, acrylic varnishes are now commonly used. Though a little less durable they are completely colourless and dry quickly. Both types of varnish can be mixed with a little colour to create tinted transparent glazes which are useful for antiquing furniture and other surfaces.

Lacquers, or shellacs, also provide a protective layer and are made from animal resin dissolved in denatured alcohol (methylated spirits). These are thinner than varnishes and dry very quickly, leaving a shiny, brittle coating. Heating processes provide different colours from pale white polish to rich, dark brown button polish. Multiple coats, gently sanded in between produce a rich, polished surface for wood such as that required for French polishing. Like varnishes, lacquers can also be used as a coloured medium and pigment or metallic powders can be mixed in for decorative painting. Lacquer is useful as a barrier between oil- and water-based techniques and can be used as a quick, intermediary sealer between layers of decorative work where any mistakes can be easily rubbed off.

Water-based paints used to create clever distressing effects – a transparent wash for the wall, one solid coat rubbed back over another on the cubboard.

Varnishes and sealants

Once paint has been applied to a surface there are many ways to protect and seal it. Just as preparation is important for the preservation of a particular effect so too is the final finishing. In some cases these finishes can have both decorative as well as protective uses. For instance button polish shellac will seal a finish at the same time as providing a rich, dark lacquered effect for the colour. Below we have taken 12 pieces of skirting painted in the same yellow latex (emulsion) to demonstrate exactly how each finish affects the colour and surface of the paint.

1 Antiquing patina, a proprietary, water-based raw umber glaze that can be applied to new paintwork or plaster to enrich and antique it

2 Boot polish, another way of antiquing new paintwork. Dark brown in colour, it creates a rich, polished finish that can be buffed up to a high shine

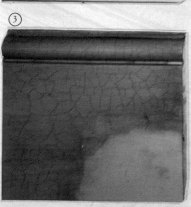

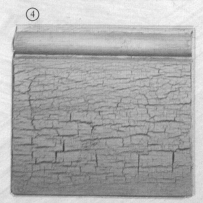

3 Craquelure, a two-varnish system where a slow-drying varnish is applied over a quick-drying varnish causing the top varnish to crack. Artist's oil paint is rubbed into the cracks to colour them

4 Crackle glaze, a thick, water-based solution that causes one water-based paint to crack over when put on top of another

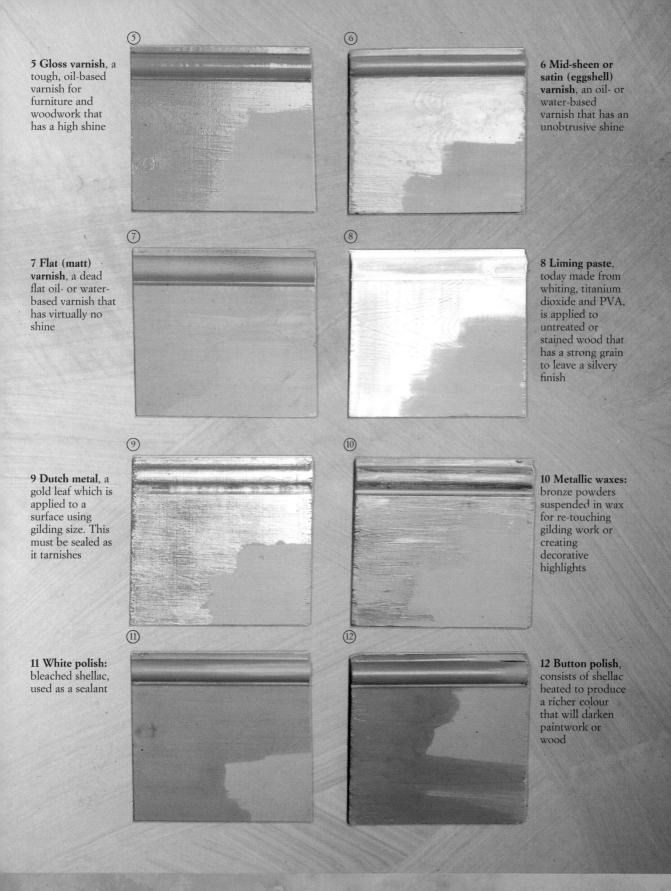

5 Gloss varnish, a tough, oil-based varnish for furniture and woodwork that has a high shine

6 Mid-sheen or satin (eggshell) varnish, an oil- or water-based varnish that has an unobtrusive shine

7 Flat (matt) varnish, a dead flat oil- or water-based varnish that has virtually no shine

8 Liming paste, today made from whiting, titanium dioxide and PVA, is applied to untreated or stained wood that has a strong grain to leave a silvery finish

9 Dutch metal, a gold leaf which is applied to a surface using gilding size. This must be sealed as it tarnishes

10 Metallic waxes: bronze powders suspended in wax for re-touching gilding work or creating decorative highlights

11 White polish: bleached shellac, used as a sealant

12 Button polish, consists of shellac heated to produce a richer colour that will darken paintwork or wood

Varnishes and sealants

TYPE	CONSTITUTION	PROPERTIES	USES
OIL-BASED POLYURETHANE VARNISH	Polyurethane alkyd, satin and flat (matt) versions have flattening agent added to diminish the natural gloss of this product	Transparent medium that is very tough and hard wearing. Available in gloss, satin and flat (matt) finishes. Gloss is the toughest. Slow drying, slightly yellow; will tend to yellow with time.	Versatile product used to protect interior and exterior surfaces. Can be used to protect paintwork and bare wood although the fumes are unpleasant if used on walls.
ACRYLIC VARNISH	Acrylic polymers, flattening agent added as above	A milky looking varnish that dries clear without any coloration. Available in gloss, satin and flat (matt) finishes. Tough enough to be used on floors. Quick drying, will not yellow with age.	Designed to directly replace oil-based equivalent. Has the advantage of being fast drying and has no unpleasant smell, although should be used with care over recently applied oil paints.
SHELLAC OR LACQUER	Shellac is derived from a tree and comes in flakes which are dissolved in alcohol	Button polish is the natural orange colour of shellac. White polish is bleached clear. Shellacs are fast drying and can be used to give a very fine finish as in french polish. Will always subsequently dissolve in its solvent, alcohol.	Shellac is used to give a very fine finish as a lacquer although it is not nearly as durable as a varnish. Decorators like it as it dries in minutes and it is useful as a barrier coat.

TYPE	CONSTITUTION	PROPERTIES	USES
STAINS	Can be either oil- or water-based. Stains are mostly water on paint thinner (white spirit), and pigment with a little binder	Very concentrated colour designed to penetrate bare wood. Traditionally meant to be varnished but now some coloured varnishes are sold as "varnish stains" which need no further protection.	Intend to make cheaper woods appear more exotic than they really are. Usually "wood" coloured, although some look rather artificial.
WAX	Waxes are derived from various sources. Carnauba wax, the hardest wax, is a plant wax; beeswax comes from bees; paraffin wax is inorganic	Waxes are mixed with turpentine to allow them to be applied easily. They can be buffed to a deep shine, depending on the type of wax. Waxes are available either almost clear or coloured as antique furniture polish or boot polish. They can have whiteners added to them as in liming wax, or metal powder to create gilt cream.	Waxes are used to protect furniture and floors. Over time they build up to an attractive patina. The can be used on bare wood or over a paint or varnish. They can also be used for techniques such as antiquing. Wax is very tough although it will dissolve in paint thinner (white spirit). Wax cannot be overpainted.
PAINT MAGIC ANTIQUING PATINA (or acrylic paint and scumble glaze)	A wax emulsified in water with added pigment	A liquid that can be brushed onto a surface. Comes in two colours, a warm brown and a cool brown. Has a degree of protective power.	Used to give an appearance of age. Applied over paintwork it is selectively abraded with wire wool when dry to imitate natural wear and tear.

Useful materials

Decorating can be an expensive business and so it is useful to gather any cost-cutting ideas. There are many materials not normally associated with decorating that can offer interesting options. For curtains and upholstery cheaper fabrics include cheesecloth (muslin) and hessian.

1 Hessian, a cheap and surprisingly versatile material that is tough and has a rough weave; ideal for making cushions or stencilled screens **2 Cotton duck canvas** can be used for creating painted floor cloths which are an economical way of covering floors **3 Regular fabric** – Try department store remnant boxes for the more expensive fabrics on the market **4 Cheesecloth (muslin)** is a delicate, transparent fabric that comes bleached or dyed and makes very pretty curtains or bed canopies. Try stencilling white paint onto white muslin to create a lacy effect. **5 Hardboard** – if you have damaged floors try covering them with sheets of hardboard and painting a design onto it

8

9

10

11

12

13

**6 Brown
paper** for parcels
has a rich, mellow
colour and can be
used as a very
economical wall covering
7 Regular wallpaper – try
historical collections for
interesting alternatives
8 Wrapping paper can make
an interesting alternative for
papering small areas
9 & 10 Sisal, a hard wearing
flooring material that has a
neutral colour and suits all
interiors **11, 12 & 13** Photocopies
can be taken from historic print
books, antiqued and applied directly
to the wall to create a print room

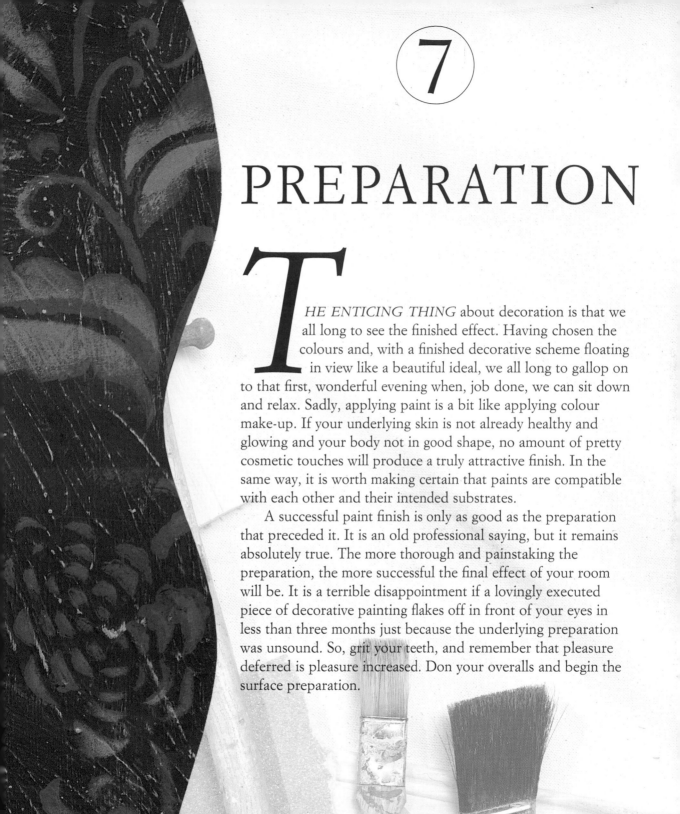

7

PREPARATION

THE ENTICING THING about decoration is that we all long to see the finished effect. Having chosen the colours and, with a finished decorative scheme floating in view like a beautiful ideal, we all long to gallop on to that first, wonderful evening when, job done, we can sit down and relax. Sadly, applying paint is a bit like applying colour make-up. If your underlying skin is not already healthy and glowing and your body not in good shape, no amount of pretty cosmetic touches will produce a truly attractive finish. In the same way, it is worth making certain that paints are compatible with each other and their intended substrates.

A successful paint finish is only as good as the preparation that preceded it. It is an old professional saying, but it remains absolutely true. The more thorough and painstaking the preparation, the more successful the final effect of your room will be. It is a terrible disappointment if a lovingly executed piece of decorative painting flakes off in front of your eyes in less than three months just because the underlying preparation was unsound. So, grit your teeth, and remember that pleasure deferred is pleasure increased. Don your overalls and begin the surface preparation.

Order of works

If you are restoring an old house or apartment, a lot of time can be saved on preparation by using skilled professionals for wiring, plastering and carpentry. If this work is done well, the amount of time you spend on filling and sanding can be cut to the minimum. A little extra money spent on the earlier stages will prove well worth while.

Once the builders have moved out, begin preparing all surfaces for decoration:

FIXTURES

It is a good idea to decide on the position of items such as light fittings, pelmets, wall cupboards and shelving, and drill the holes for them before painting begins. If you try to drill them after painting is finished, there is a danger that newly painted surfaces will be damaged, should you get their position wrong or approach the job clumsily. Many paint effects cannot be touched up successfully.

WALLS AND CEILINGS

The best surface for most paint finishes is a sound, smooth wall. If your walls fit this description you are very fortunate as the bulk of the initial work involved in preparation is getting your walls into this state.

Wallpapers require particular types of treatment. Old wallpaper can be painted over if it is sound and well stuck down. If the odd edge is loose it can be stuck down with seam adhesive otherwise if the paper is coming adrift in large areas it is probably better to strip it and start again. Plastic-coated wallpapers do not accept paint well, especially latex (emulsion) paint, and should be stripped. Papers made from vinyl can be painted quite successfully. Textured wallpaper can be painted over if you like the texture, and textured wallpaper below a chair rail (dado rail) can look good if painted the same colour as the walls above; an attractive pattern can help break up a large wall area.

Preparation plan

1. The ceiling should be completed before the wall and floor are tackled. Paint in strips parallel to the window wall, working away from the light. Make sure your stepladder is perfectly stable and always lay dropcloths or dust sheets below. A roller and tray are the speediest tools to use.

2. Next, using a roller paint the walls from the top downwards, again working away from the light. Use brushes or small rollers to cut in around doorways and windows, the top of baseboards (skirting boards), and for painting in the four corners of the room and the top of the walls. A radiator brush is helpful for reaching behind central heating pipes.

3. Paint all woodwork with a 1½ in (40 mm) brush to ensure sharp, neat edges. Take care that all surfaces are painted; it is easy to miss a section of door or window frame, particularly in the case of sash windows.

4. Lastly treat the floor. If you are painting it make sure you begin in the farthest corner, working backwards towards the door so you do not become trapped. Once complete close the door and allow no activity to take place there until it is thoroughly dry.

You may have walls covered in woodchip, a lumpy paper which most people will encounter at some stage. It looks fairly awful and nothing really disguises the "lumpy porridge" look successfully so it may be better to remove it. A word of caution is needed here: woodchip is often used to conceal dreadful, crumbling walls – something it does rather well – so be prepared for a lot of work if you do decide to strip it off.

Textured coating is another difficulty you might well encounter; it is usually found on ceilings although some people get carried away and cover their walls as well. Gentle swirls on ceilings can be sanded off although be very careful as older types of textured coating contained asbestos which must not be inhaled under any circumstances. You can try soaking the coating with water; if you are lucky it might soften and can then be scraped off. Bad textured-coating stalactites can be skimmed with a layer of plaster to conceal them. (If you are plastering a ceiling it is a good idea to wear goggles.) If your home has had the full "texture" treatment and the walls look rough, this is probably the reason why it was applied in the first place. In the long term it will be easier to have all the offending areas stripped and replastered. You can tell if there is old distemper on the plasterwork as it comes off on a damp cloth and it should be scrubbed off as neither paper nor modern paint adheres to it satisfactorily.

Walls in Good Condition

Walls that are in good condition should be washed down with an all-purpose cleaner or sugar soap solution and rinsed with clean water. Any knocks or dents in the wall should be filled with a plaster spackle (filler). Use one that you mix with water, rather than using the ready-mixed ones which are harder to sand and more expensive. When the spackle (filler) has dried, sand it flush with the wall using a medium-grade sandpaper and dust down the walls with a dusting brush. The walls are now ready for painting.

Stripping Old Wallpaper

Old paper is stripped more easily using a wallpaper stripper. This is really a giant kettle with a hose leading to a metal plate which is held against the wall. The heat and moisture soften the wallpaper paste and it becomes easier to scrape off the paper. Unless the old paper is falling off the wall it is well worth the modest cost to hire this equipment. Plastic-coated paper or paper that has been painted with oil-based paint will need to be either slashed with a knife or keyed using a wallpaper perforator, a vicious-looking metal-spiked roller that perforates the paper before the wallpaper stripper is used. (Perforators can also be hired.)

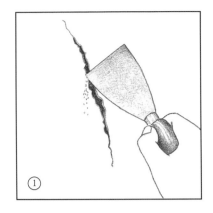

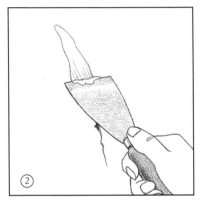

1. Before filling the crack dislodge any loose material from it using a filling knife and then dust it out thoroughly.

2. Scrape a small amount of spackle (filler) into the crack so that it is slightly proud of the surface.

3. When dry wrap some medium grade sandpaper around a sanding block and rub back the spackle (filler)

Once the old paper has been removed go over the walls again to ensure any little flecks of paper that you missed the first time round are cleaned off. Take stock of the condition of the plasterwork, but do not panic if the walls look a mess as old plaster usually does. The main thing to check is that the plaster is sound. Check this by tapping the walls with your knuckles and listening for a hollow sound; this indicates that the plaster has become detached from the wall or "blown". Inevitably there will be a few small areas of blown plaster in an old house and these can be disregarded. If the blown plaster extends over a considerable area and is accompanied by large cracks it is time to call in the plasterers. Any damp areas should be investigated for their cause and appropriate remedial work carried out. Damp-affected plaster should be removed and new plaster applied. Waterproofing products that seal the wall are best avoided as they will only mask the effect and not cure the underlying problem.

Small dents and cracks revealed once the wallpaper has been stripped can be filled with a plaster-based spackle (filler) but do not worry about filling fine cracks as liner (lining) paper will disguise these. Lumps and ridges are more of a problem as these always show up on the finished wall. If they cannot be sanded down try filling around them so that they present a smoother profile and are therefore less obvious. An orbital sander will save time although it will throw up clouds of dust. It is advisable to wear a dust mask whenever you are sanding. Dust the walls down with a soft brush and clean all the dust from the room.

LINING THE WALLS

Liner (lining) paper is a heavy-grade plain paper that is excellent for covering a multitude of sins. It is usually used over bare plaster unless the plaster is new or in pristine condition. Begin by sizing the walls using a diluted wallpaper paste made up following the manufacturer's instructions. Cut the paper so

Preparation materials

Although it can be tedious, beginners must not begrudge time spent on preparation and should realize that a well-prepared finish can last up to three or four times longer than if applied to an unsound surface. It is wise to keep a constant stock of the basic materials at hand, such as stripping solutions, fillers, abrasive materials such as sandpapers and wire wools, and primers.

1. Acrylic primer, for new wood and old painted surfaces

2. Red oxide metal primer, for use on all metals

3. Tinted plastic wood – this comes in a range of colours to match different woods. It drives very hard and so is particularly suitable for filling floors

5. Gesso powder, to be made up into white gesso

4. Instant spackle (filler) – available in a tube and ideal for filling cracks and holes

6. All-purpose cleaner (sugar soap), used for cleaning surfaces prior to applying paint effects

7. Oil-based tile primer which makes possible the application of paint effects onto old or ugly tiles

⑦

⑧

8. Shellac, or knotting: used for sealing the resinous knots in new wood and preventing them from staining the paint finish

⑨

⑩

10. Acrylic primer, a water-based primer which is perfect for preparing laminates for paint effects

9. Paint and varnish stripper, for removing old paint, varnish or shellacs

⑪

⑫

⑬

12. Denatured alcohol (methylated spirit). used with wire wool to remove old shellacs and lacquers

11. Ready-mixed acrylic gesso, for priming surfaces for fine hand painting or gilding

13. Acrylic modelling paste, a high-build paste used to fill cracks and to create raised patterns on the surface of objects ready for gilding or painting

that it is about 4 in (10 cm) longer than the height of the wall. Lay the paper flat on a pasting table or other flat surface and apply the wallpaper paste generously, making sure the edges are also pasted. Loosely fold the paper (without creasing it) taking both ends into the middle. Allow the paper to stand until damp.

To hang the first drop, start papering from one corner and allow ¼ in (6 mm) of paper to pass around the corner to create a neat join later. Never leave more than ¼ in (6 mm) as the paper will probably kink or become detached from the wall at a later date. Peel back the top portion of pasted paper and, standing on a stepladder, hold the paper against the wall allowing a 2 in (5 cm) excess to overlap on the ceiling area. Working your way down the wall, smooth out any air bubbles and excess paste using a wallpapering brush. When you are halfway down the wall lift the bottom portion of the drop away from the wall and peel away the last bit of paper which has been hanging pasted sides together.

Continue smoothing out the paper, working down to the level of the baseboard (skirting board). You should be left with a 2 in (5 cm) excess of paper overlapping the board. Mark the excess paper at both ceiling and baseboard (skirting board) level with the back of the blade of a pair of paper-hanging scissors. Peel it back and trim along the marked line for a neat finish.

Line across the wall, butting the paper as you go (avoid overlapping the paper as this leaves unsightly joins). Any gaps between the paper can easily be filled and lightly sanded for a perfect finish. The paper should be allowed to dry overnight before painting.

Serious irregularities in the wall's surface can be masked by "cross-lining" i.e., hanging the paper in horizontal strips and then, when the first layer is dry, hanging a second layer of paper in the normal vertical fashion.

Liner (lining) paper should be primed with a coat of diluted flat latex (matt emulsion) paint to seal it. When the paint is dry, you are ready to begin applying colour.

LINING A WALL

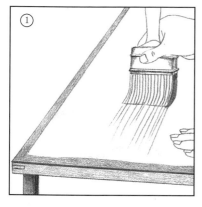

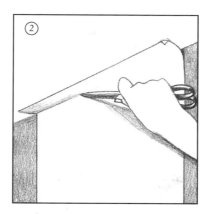

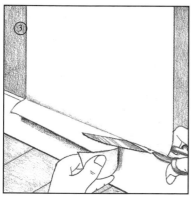

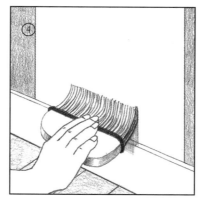

1. Cut a length of liner (lining) paper that is a little longer than the height of the wall and lay it face down on a pasting board or other stable surface. Use a wide wallpaper brush to apply a thin film of wallpaper adhesive. Brush this out evenly making sure there are no lumps in the paste.

2. When the paper is damp all over, position it on the wall, starting at the top, allowing it to overlap the ceiling and base board (skirting board) a little. Use scissors to score it at top and bottom to indicate where it should be cut (see Lining the Walls p.91 for more details).

3. Use long, sharp paper scissors to cut off the overlap. Be careful not to pull or tear the paper as it will be soft and moist.

4. Use a dry wallpaper brush to smooth out the paper and ensure it has adhered properly with no air bubbles or lumps of paste behind it.

Prime and undercoat the woodwork if required. If you are using oil-based paint on the woodwork and water-based paint on the walls try to avoid getting the oil-based paint on the liner (lining) paper. Otherwise, if you colourwash the walls over a matt latex paint or emulsion at a later date the colourwash will soak into the emulsion but not into the oil paint on the walls, producing an annoying patchy effect. Paint the walls and ceiling, then paint all the woodwork with the top coats. Once these are completed, fit or re-fit the fixtures for which holes were drilled at the start of the work.

Woodwork

Before beginning to prepare your woodwork for painting, think about the final paint finish you want to apply. Most paint finishes look much better if the woodwork is smooth and blemish-free, however an antiqued paint finish would look more convincing if the surface is a bit rough to begin with – which is good news if you have old woodwork and do not relish the prospect of all the filling and sanding needed to achieve, say, a marbled finish.

Unless you have had recent carpentry work done you will almost certainly be confronted with previously painted woodwork if the woodwork has not been stripped already. If you do have what appears to be stripped wood, first take a dampened rag with a little paint thinner (white spirit) and wipe it over the surface. If a brown residue comes off the wood has been waxed and it is vital that the wax is removed before any further preparation takes place. This can be done by wiping over the surface with a rag soaked in paint thinner (white spirit) which will dissolve the wax finish. Repeat this procedure two or three times to ensure every last trace of wax is removed. In case any of the wax has soaked into the wood and cannot be removed it might be better to finish off using oil-based paints which are less likely to flake off. If the wood has been varnished rather than waxed treat it in the same way as previously painted woodwork (see next page).

STAINED WOOD

Stained wood needs treating with care as the stain can bleed through and discolour subsequent coats of paint. If you are using a colour that is paler than the stain colour try painting it onto a small section and allow to dry before decorating the whole area. If it changes colour try using the opposite type of paint, for example if an oil-based satin or eggshell paint changes colour it is likely that a water-based one will not. Failing that, use an aluminium primer (a particularly tough, though expensive, paint) over the stain.

The thorough preparation of woodwork is essential, however simple the finish. The constant activity that takes place in this kitchen will quickly affect the paintwork if it has been applied to a dirty or unsanded surface.

Previously Painted Woodwork

Woodwork that has been painted previously would almost certainly have been painted using an oil-based paint. Provided the paintwork is reasonably smooth wash it down with an all-purpose cleaner or sugar soap solution and then rinse with clean water. Sand using a medium grade sandpaper such as an aluminium oxide paper to roughen the surface to provide a key for the new paint and also to remove any "nibs" (raised areas). Fill any small knocks or dents with a plaster spackle (filler) and sand level. Large holes and gaps where the wood is jointed should be filled with a wood spackle (filler) as this is very tough and will not crack or fall out. Do not overfill as wood spackle (filler) is difficult to sand. Fine cracks on joints and panel mouldings can be filled with a flexible decorator's spackle (filler) applied with a caulking gun and wiped smooth with a cloth while still wet. Dust down the surface, which is now ready for painting.

Stripping Old Paintwork

Older properties that have not been extensively modernized frequently contain woodwork that is characterized by a lumpy orange-peel appearance with old paint dribbles and blurry, indistinct mouldings. This is due to a thick layer of paint where the woodwork has been repainted many times. It is almost impossible to create a decent surface for painting on so the only sensible course is to strip the paint and start again.

There are two ways of stripping old paintwork, using either a chemical method or heat. Using heat is the quickest and cheapest method: the paint is melted using a blowtorch or a hot air paint stripper, a tool that resembles a hairdrier. When using this method, start at the bottom of the area to be stripped as hot air rises, and play the heat source over the paint until it bubbles. Scrape off the melted paint using a triangular scraper or shavehook. Take care when doing this as the paint that is being removed is hot and may blister the skin. Always wear protective

Painting a Door

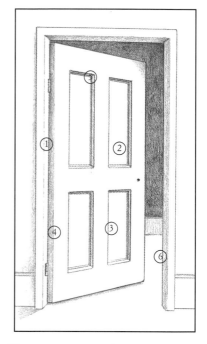

There is an art to applying paint to doors. Follow the order of work indicated here. Use a 1½ in (40 mm) brush and make sure that the bristles get right into the corners. Paint designed for woodwork is very thick to withstand wear and tear and must be brushed out evenly using vertical and then horizontal brush strokes.
1. Rebates
2. Mouldings of panels
3. Inside panel
4. Verticals
5. Horizontals
6. Door Frame

gloves and goggles. Old paint is often lead-based and therefore toxic. It can cause an allergic reaction in some people so, when removing old paintwork, always work in a well-ventilated area and wear hand and eye protection. Large flat areas are easy to strip but mouldings require greater care as they are easily scorched. You might prefer to use chemical strippers to treat intricate areas. Be very careful of fire: always use old drop cloths or dust sheets (which can be slightly dampened) to catch the paint droppings and keep an eye on them as it is all too easy for a smouldering sheet to burst into flames at your feet. Good ventilation is very important. Open the windows to allow plenty of air to circulate; items such as doors can be taken off their hinges and stripped outside if the weather permits. Most areas of woodwork can be stripped using heat although windows are best stripped using chemicals due to the risk of the glass cracking. When all the paint has been stripped sand the surface smooth; sanding will also remove any remaining paint residue.

The chemical method of stripping is usually reserved for intricate areas of paintwork (such as mouldings) and for woodwork that is to be left stripped as there is no risk of the wood scorching. Paint stripper has a gel-like consistency to enable it to cling to vertical surfaces. Brush a generous layer onto the surface to be stripped using an old paint brush and leave it for up to 20 minutes to react. Once it has softened the old paintwork, scrape off the paint layer using a triangular scraper or shavehook. When all the paint has been removed neutralize the chemical according to the manufacturer's recommendations, usually water or denatured alcohol (methylated spirit). Portable items can be dipped by specialist companies; refer to p.107 (the Furniture section) for further details.

You may prefer a transparent colour for your woodwork that stains the wood but reveals the grain. This will necessitate completely stripping the surface of any old paint or varnish, as well as the application of at least two coats of a varnish afterwards.

These cupboards demonstrate a clever way of retaining the beauty of good-quality, untreated wood while linking the piece to the rest of the decorative scheme with a simple border of matching colour.

Repainting woodwork that has been stripped involves similar treatment to new woodwork. Dab some shellac (knotting) on to any knots to prevent seepage of sap left in the wood as this can cause discoloration and lifting of the subsequent paint layers. Fill any holes and cracks as described on p.98 and sand smooth. Apply a coat of wood primer. You may find the whiteness of the primer reveals a lot of minor imperfections which can be now filled using a fine-grade surface spackle (filler). Sand down the whole area to smooth the spackle (filler) and the woodgrain which will have been raised by the primer. The woodwork is now ready for the finishing coats (modern wood primers usually double up as undercoats too).

Floors

The floors of a house offer a wide range of opportunities for decoration; they usually represent the largest area for decorative colour so a paint effect underfoot can radically alter the feel and look of a space. Floors are also subject to very heavy wear and tear, and therefore great care must be taken in the preparation. Old floors that appear to be beyond repair can be transformed into something spectacular with no more preparatory work than crumbling walls covered in woodchip paper. Floors are usually made from wood: pine boards were used in older houses, while newer houses and some modernized old houses sometimes have chipboard or plywood floors; apartment blocks and some houses have concrete floors. All can be successfully painted if they are prepared correctly.

WOODEN FLOORS

Most older houses have pine boards which may have often sustained damage during earlier building work. These floors have sometimes been painted or stained around the edge and are usually very dirty. The first thing to do is to repair any physical damage. Boards that are cracked or have sections missing from them should be replaced. Floor boards are quite cheap to buy and easy to lay, but if a transparent finish is required the new boards will usually be a very different colour to the old as pine darkens with age. In this case try to obtain reclaimed boards from an architectural salvage company; otherwise use new boards and stain them to match the colour of the old boards before painting the whole floor. Damaged boards can be levered up using a bolster chisel, taking care not to spoil the board you are levering against. Cut the replacement board to length and nail in place using either 2 in (5 cm) flooring brads or cut nails, taking great care not to nail through any

If you have original floor boards, save the cost of carpeting and choose from a variety of paint effects, from checks to stencilled designs. The soft checks above are a perfect way of introducing colour within the safe confines of a formal design.

pipes or electric cables. It is rather difficult to do much about gaps between the boards, and it is best to ignore them unless wind comes whistling through or the gaps are very wide. If the gaps are not too wide they can be filled with papier-mâché although you should ensure that the sides of the boards are clean first. Wider gaps can be filled with wooden fillets cut to size; otherwise the only other alternative is to lift all the boards and move them along so they butt up against each other. The resulting gap can be filled with a new board.

TRANSPARENT FINISHES

Provided the boards are not covered in paint, stains or waxes, and are in good condition, you should scrub them clean at least twice using water. Any stubborn marks can be removed using sandpaper. If they have been waxed, the wax should be cleaned off by wiping over the boards with paint thinner (white spirit) on a rag. If the boards have been painted, you will need to sand them to remove the paint and also to eliminate all the dents and scrapes most boards will have accumulated over the years. Sanding will also level cupped or bowed and warped boards and provide a smooth surface for painting.

Begin by hammering all protruding nails with a nail punch. Specialist floor sanders can be hired; these consist of a drum sander for the bulk of the floor and a smaller disk sander for the edges. Always follow the manufacturer's instructions for these machines and use the dust mask and ear defenders supplied with the machine. The bulk of the work is achieved with the coarsest grade of paper, which will level cupped boards and also remove old paint and stains, provided these have not penetrated the wood too deeply. Finish off with the finer grades of paper and thoroughly clean all the dust from the room before painting. If the wood is very dark it can be lightened using a wood bleach, which is either a strong acid or alkali. Follow the manufacturer's instructions carefully and wear rubber gloves and goggles. Try the wood bleach on a small area first as it can

If your boards are in particularly good condition you may prefer a transparent finish. The rich tones of wood certainly add warmth to a room. If you have new, pale-coloured boards try tinting your varnish to stain them.

sometimes make the wood change to an undesirable colour such as yellow (although this is usually only a problem if the wood has been previously stained). Once the bleaching has been carried out neutralize the chemical again following the manufacturer's instructions and allow to dry before painting.

Opaque Finishes

Opaque finishes are useful as they will cover all old paint, stains, and general marks. Before applying them ensure all wax is removed and thoroughly scrub the boards with clean water. The worst of the dents and cracks can be filled with a wood spackle (filler) and sanded level. Woodwash will cover old boards very effectively although previously painted areas should be primed first with water-based acrylic primer. If you wish to paint the floor with conventional paint treat the knots with shellac (knotting), prime the bare wood then follow with the top coats.

Chipboard and Plywood

These can be treated in the same way as wooden floor boards except any sanding should be done with a belt sander and care should be taken not to remove too much material. Chipboard is never going to give anything other than a very rough finish and if any grease has been spilt onto it this will prove impossible to remove as it will have soaked in; this will cause subsequent paint layers to flake off. Consider covering chipboard with sheets of ¼ in (6 mm) plywood and then painting colour on top of that.

Linoleum and Vinyl

If these coverings are worn or damaged, they should be removed before painting as the paint effect will not be even in these areas. Normally you can just pull them away to reveal the original flooring substrate which should be dealt with according to the material. If the vinyl has been stuck down the main problem will be removing the glue residue which can be fairly tough. A combination of patient sanding and scraping is the only effective method of removal.

Tiles

Although tiles can be painted with special tile primers (without which the paint will not withstand heavy wear and tear and will quickly chip off), if you choose to remove them do so with care as there is a high risk of damaging the substrate, and a lot of remedial work is usually required. The tiles can be removed using a bolster chisel and spalling (club) hammer, but if the tiles are particularly well fixed hire an electric rotary hammer with interchangeable bits. Whichever method of removal you choose always wear goggles and ear defenders. Tiles are normally fixed onto a cement floor or rigid plywood. Once you have removed the tiles, the tile adhesive should be chipped away using scrapers and the surface repaired. If the substrate is cement this is easily filled by simply mixing up some new cement and filling the damaged areas using a plasterer's float to smooth the cement level. Plywood can be filled with wood spackle (filler) and sanded smooth when dry.

Cement

Painting cement is an excellent way of brightening up the otherwise dull surface. If necessary the surface should first be filled using cement mixed with water; for small areas dry, ready-mixed sand and cement can be bought in small bags from builder's merchants. For larger areas, or if the entire surface is so rough that it requires skimming, buy the sand and cement separately. The surface may take several weeks to cure depending on the atmospheric conditions. For a paint finish such as marbling or a faux stone look paint the surface white, priming the cement with an alkali-resisting primer followed by an undercoat and two coats of satin or eggshell paint. Proprietary floor paint can be painted onto the bare surface. The colours may need intermixing as the range is not exciting.

Furniture

Old furniture can still be picked up quite cheaply from garage sales or markets and is transformed by painting. Modern furniture with a cheap-looking surface or knotty pine also benefits from paint treatment. Much of what is said above about preparing woodwork applies equally to furniture. The main difference is that furniture usually presents a smaller surface area than the woodwork in a room and often benefits from more intricate decorative schemes. This usually means that greater effort and care are necessary for preparing furniture for painting. Furniture usually has either a previously painted or a natural wood surface that has been enhanced and protected using a wax, varnish or french polish.

PREVIOUSLY PAINTED FURNITURE

Previously painted furniture can be painted over if the existing paintwork is sound and not chipped. Wash the piece down thoroughly with an all-purpose cleaner or sugar soap solution and rinse carefully with clean water. Sand the surface with a fine-grade paper, taking care not to flatten mouldings and round off corners. Fill any small knocks and dents with a plaster spackle (filler) and sand level. Large holes and gaps where the wood is jointed should be filled with a wood spackle (filler) and sanded smooth. Dust down the surface ready for painting. It is safest to assume the old paint was an oil-based paint; if you want to apply a water-based paint such as woodwash you will first need to apply a water-based acrylic primer. For a paint finish that requires a satin or eggshell sheen you must undercoat the piece first then apply two coats of satin or eggshell paint, sanding between coats for a perfect finish.

Preparation for ornately decorated pieces, such as the Chinoiserie cupboard above, must be particularly thorough. Use silicon carbide (wet-and-dry) paper between coats of primer and undercoat to achieve a very smooth finish for hand painting.

STRIPPING OLD PAINT AND VARNISH

If the paint on the piece of furniture is in any way unsound or is lumpy and uneven it is usually better to strip it off and start again. Due to the small scale of most pieces the stripping process is relatively quick and is a certain way of obtaining a perfect finish. Strip off the old paint as described in the woodwork section on pp.98-99 or have the item dipped by a specialist stripping company. A stripping company will dip the piece in a tank of paint stripper and return it to you ready to paint, so cutting out a lot of work, especially if the piece has intricate mouldings and areas that are awkward to reach using a triangular scraper or shavehook. Bear in mind that different companies use various types of paint stripper, some of which can damage the wood. Caustic soda is a notable example: it causes the wood to shrink which opens up the joints and the wood becomes "whiskery" and dry. Other types of stripper are benign and fine hardwood pieces can come back looking like new. Always check what the company are using to strip the paint before committing yourself.

WAXED AND POLISHED FURNITURE

All wax should be removed as described in the woodwork section on p.97. Varnished wood must be thoroughly sanded or stripped before painting and french polish should also be sanded or stripped. French polish is very easy to remove as it dissolves in denatured alcohol (methylated spirit). Go over the piece with the denatured alcohol (methylated spirit) on fine wire wool in the same way as removing old wax. Once the old finish has been removed, sand to remove any residue before painting.

REPAIRING THE SURFACE

Veneer that has lifted can be stuck down with wood glue or cut out and filled. Fill the holes and cracks using a wood spackle (filler). An alternative way of achieving a top class finish is to gesso the piece after filling the worst of the craters. Gesso is

Original pieces can be restored prior to filling in with gesso, a mixture of rabbit-skin glue and whiting which will fill in any cracks and smooth out any dents before being sanded to an immaculate finish.

made from a mixture of rabbit-skin glue and whiting. The glue can be bought from artist's suppliers in the form of granules. Cover half a cup of granules with water and soak overnight. The following day put the softened granules into a double boiler and add 2 cups of hot water and stir over a low heat until the granules have dissolved. Sift (sieve) the whiting and slowly add it, little by little, to the mixture, and stir to disperse. Continue adding the whiting until the mixture assumes a thin creamy texture. Brush the warm gesso over the bare wood and allow to dry for a couple of hours. Sand the gesso smooth and apply a further coat of gesso, brushing on at right angles to the first coat. Sand lightly until smooth, taking care not to remove too much material from corners and raised mouldings. Continue to apply the gesso and sand until you have built up at least five coats. The surface should now be as smooth as glass and ready for the application of the top coats. Adding gesso to a piece requires a considerable amount of time and skill and you may not be inclined to go to so much trouble. A faster and easier, although more expensive, method is to use acrylic gesso which can be bought ready to apply from an artist's suppliers. A cheaper alternative is acrylic primer for wood. This is quite thick and very tough and both alternatives should be applied in the same way as the traditional gesso.

PAINTING THE SURFACE

The piece of furniture is now ready for painting. Refer to the woodwork section for guidance on painting. It is better to use undercoat on woodwork that has not been gessoed in addition to the standard primer/undercoat as this will help to build up a finer surface. Use a silicon carbide (wet-and-dry) paper to sand between finishing coats; this is a very tough paper that comes in fine grades and is usually used wet as the water stops the paper clogging up. Dip the paper periodically in a bucket of water to keep it lubricated. Wipe the surface clean and allow to dry before applying the paint.

Other surfaces

There are other types of material to which you might want to apply paint; the suitability of the material in question for painting and the necessary steps required to prime the surface for painting are described below.

METAL

Metal accepts paint very well. Oil-based paint can be applied successfully to previously painted metal although it is important to carry out a patch test first to see whether the new paint reacts with the old. If in doubt remove the old paint using chemical stripper, an easy task since it is almost impossible to damage metal by heavy-handed scraping unless the metal in question is a soft aluminium alloy. Old, rusted metal should first be treated with a proprietary rust killer. Use a wire brush to remove the loose rust and apply the rust killer according to the manufacturer's instructions. Any pitting or dents can be filled with car body spackle (filler) and sanded level. Prime the bare metal with a rust-inhibiting metal primer. Metal primer is always oil-based as water-based paint would cause bare metal to rust. If you want to use water-based paints apply a coat of water-based acrylic primer first, otherwise use an oil-based undercoat followed by the top coats.

PLASTIC

Painting plastic is a slightly hit-and-miss affair as there are so many different types of plastics that will either accept or repel paint according to the kind of plastic. You are most likely to encounter the types of plastic that are commonly found in the home:

LAMINATES

Plastic laminates are commonly used to face kitchen cabinets and cupboards. They can be satisfactorily painted to transform what can be a garish and cheap-looking surface. Preparation is very straightforward and involves sanding the laminate using a fine-grade silicon carbide (wet-and-dry) paper used wet to minutely roughen and key the surface. Fine-grade wire wool can be used as an alternative although silicon carbide (wet-and-dry) paper does have the advantage of being dust-free if used wet. The surface must be washed down and painted with an oil-based undercoat followed by the top coats; alternatively prime the laminate with water-based acrylic primer and follow with a water-based paint. Bear in mind that although paint will stick to these plastics it can chip off if subjected to heavy wear and tear; worktops should never be painted.

PLASTIC FLOWER POTS AND GARDEN FURNITURE

Flower pots and garden furniture are made from softer plastics and can be painted although the paint may eventually flake or chip off if any flexing of the item occurs. The paint will adhere to the plastic more satisfactorily if it is flamed first. This involves passing a blowtorch very briefly over the surface. Under no circumstances must the plastic be allowed to melt; the idea is to break down the mould-release agents which are used in the manufacture of the plastic then abrade the surface with silicon carbide (wet-and-dry) paper and paint as for laminates.

CERAMIC TILES AND GLASS

Removing ceramic tiles is a tough job and more and more people are opting to paint them. The paint cannot bind well to non-absorbent, smooth surfaces and will chip off very easily so it is best to prime the tiles with a tile primer, which is an oil-based paint, and then paint with the top coats. An alternative is to paint onto the tiles using a special tile or glass paint or mix colours into a suitable varnish. Tile primer and varnish are elastic when dry and this means that they are less likely to chip off. Bear in mind that while you can paint these materials they will not withstand heavy wear and tear. The exception to this is unglazed terracotta which takes paint very well with no preparation because of its absorbency.

PROTECTING THE SURFACE

Once the paint finish has been completed a coat of varnish will considerably extend its life, especially in areas that will see a lot of use and in rooms that are subject to high levels of moisture. Woodwork should always be given a coat of varnish, either a polyurethane varnish thinned with a little paint thinner (white spirit) to help prevent yellowing or an acrylic varnish used neat. The same can be used on walls although you should always leave an oil-based finish for a week or two to ensure it is fully dry and cured before applying an acrylic varnish.

REVARNISHING

Eventually some decorated areas will begin to wear through. Prompt action is vital to avoid further, preventable deterioration. Try to touch up the damaged area using a matching colour applied with a small artist's brush. Once it has dried, wash the area down with an all-purpose cleaner or sugar soap solution and rinse. When dry, re-varnish the whole section where deterioration has taken place, or even the whole room if necessary. Try to use the same type of varnish that was used in the first instance.

TOUCHING UP DAMAGED AREAS

If the damage to a finish is limited a small repair is unlikely to show up much and will nearly always be preferable to repainting the whole area. Physical damage should be filled using a plaster-board spackle (filler). Instead of allowing it to dry and then sanding the areas, thereby causing more damage, you should smooth the repair when it is semi-dry using a damp sponge until it is level with the surrounding area. Once the filler is completely dry apply the base-coat paint to the repair using a small artist's brush, taking care not to get paint beyond the damaged area. Lastly, apply the final colour. You may have to make this colour a little more concentrated than the original and dot it on carefully until it blends in with the surrounding colour.

THE PROJECTS

O VER THE NEXT four chapters we will be introducing you to the more stunning yet straightforward decorative paint techniques, and demonstrating how recent developments in paint technology have influenced interior design. To achieve this we took four regular rooms from a real home – sitting room, kitchen, bathroom, bedroom – and demonstrated how they were transformed completely. These rooms were in varying states of disrepair – some had not been used for many years – and so needed considerable attention.

The techniques shown can be adapted to suit any interior. The effects are very varied, ranging from those suitable for large scale projects such an overall stencilled scheme for walls to those applied to small, decorative accessories. To guarantee stylistic variation different themes were chosen for each room – from warm, exotic tones for the bathroom to cool but sweet Scandinavian colours for the bedroom. Each technique has been introduced with a little background information as well as general advice, together with illustrated step-by-step sequences and a complete list of materials. Do not be afraid of varying your own styles and choice of effects; use the projects for inspiration as well as instruction.

Look hard at the pictures and refer back to the "before" shots to see just how easy it is to transform something with paint. You may have something similar at home that you never dreamed could be so handsome.

THE
SITTING
ROOM

OF THE FOUR rooms we decided to transform, the sitting room probably presented the fewest problems. We were very lucky to inherit attractive features: the wonderfully high ceiling and a whole wall of tall sash windows that caught the afternoon sun, and the feelings of spaciousness and light. An original fireplace, though boarded up, provided a good focal point, as did the deep baseboards (skirting boards) and floor boards, which were in surprisingly good condition.

Only the walls had to be filled and re-lined. Once the walls had been prepared, and the woodwork sanded and primed, we were able to apply some relatively simple but nonetheless exciting diverse paint effects.

To emphasize the afternoon sun, we decided on a bright scheme of yellow with pale green and soft red details.

Colourwash stripes

The colourwash technique is a great favourite in the world of décor. It can be applied speedily, allowing you to transform your room in just a couple of hours and it is probably the most relaxed version of broken colour work that seems to suit any interior. The application of transparent washes of colour over large areas has a long history and Italian fresco techniques of the early Renaissance inspired me to formulate my own version of colourwash painting. It has a marvellous ability to re-activate dull, opaque wall finishes and add warmth and light to gloomy interiors. Its versatility is enormous: dramatic, visible brushstrokes can add immediate animation and depth to a bland, two-dimensional surface, while soft, circular sponge movements will achieve a more gentle, calming veil of colour. It can be used in a formal way, such as the stripes shown here, or it can present the perfect background for stencilling. It is an extremely economical way of decorating your walls and it can be achieved very successfully by a complete beginner.

In terms of materials needed, there are several recipes available for both water- and oil-based colourwashing methods. Some professionals simply dilute a regular emulsion and apply it to their prepared ground. Others use historical materials such as distemper washes but these inevitably entail a lot of time spent colour mixing and hunting for authentic ingredients. For beginners it is often a good idea to try one of the proprietary colourwashes available, as these have a built-in retardant that will slow the drying process, so allowing more time for manipulation.

One of the most important elements in achieving the colourwash effect is the preparation. Damaged walls must be filled and then primed and sealed with the appropriate base paint: latex (emulsion), preferably in a silk finish if using a water-based method, and a

MATERIALS AND EQUIPMENT

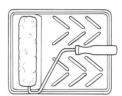
paint roller
paint tray

paint brush

acrylic primer

cream latex
(emulsion) paint,
silk finish
Buff Colourwash or
other colourwash
paint

paint kettle

large synthetic
household sponge

pencil

tape measure
or ruler

plumb line

low-tack
masking tape

Apricot Colourwash
or other colourwash
paint

damp cloth (if
needed)

flat (matt)
acrylic varnish

To ensure crisp, straight lines for our stripes we used a plumb line and chalk to create vertical marks.

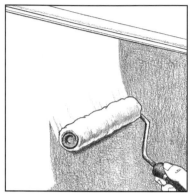

STEP 1 Prepare the walls as necessary and, using a roller, apply a coat of acrylic primer. When dry, apply a coat of cream latex (emulsion) paint. Use one that has a silk finish to prevent the colourwash paint from being absorbed too quickly.

STEP 2 Decant the colourwash paint and apply it to the wall using the household sponge. Work in wide, generous strokes starting at the top left-hand corner and moving across the wall in gentle, cloud-like shapes. Leave to dry for 24 hours.

STEP 3 Make light pencil marks at 12 in (30 cm) intervals along the top of the wall (in this case along the picture rail) and suspend the plumb line from these to create even, vertical lines from top to bottom. Mask off the divisions between stripes using low-tack masking tape.

JOCASTA'S TIP

If you would like to drag woodwork that has been painted in an oil-based paint, try adding a little detergent to the colourwash; this should avoid the need for mixing an oil-based glaze.

STEP 4 Decant the apricot colourwash. Gently sponge on alternate stripes. Take care not to paint over the edges of the masking tape, but if this happens gently wipe away the excess paint with a damp cloth. Leave the paint to dry thoroughly. Peel away the masking tape and apply a coat of 23at (matt) acrylic varnish.

satin or mid-sheen (eggshell) if using an oil-based method. Even if you have the appropriate base paint already on your wall, never try to colourwash onto unwashed walls as the grease and dust that inevitably build up in any household will prevent the solution gliding over and adhering to the surface.

When applying colourwash always finish a wall completely before stopping as you may end up with a dry edge that will be difficult to blend in later. Movements, whether with a brush or sponge should be wide and generous and your progress across the wall should be made in abstract shapes, rather than in vertical columns, as this avoids overlap marks which may build up in a regimented pattern. It is always a good idea to have a practice run, perhaps on a patch under the stairs or on a prepared board.

When deciding on colour remember that colourwash does not have to go onto a white base although this is perfectly acceptable. White tends to cool and thin colours and it is the pastel shades that will give a richness to the particular colourwash hue. Any number of combinations can be tried but the general rule is that colourwash must go over a lighter shade of itself, although pale shades are useful in softening colours that are too dark or intense. Here a rich cream is used as a base colour which gives the apricot and buff stripes a head-start in achieving their spectacular warmth.

Stripes in strong colours are a useful decorative device for concealing walls that are rough or damaged.

Checkered floor

When decorating, it is often the floor area that either raises most difficulties or is forgotten altogether. Old floors may be in a bad state of repair and yet the thought of concealing them with new carpet or tiles can bring real financial worries. Paint can be the answer, with an amazing range of possible finishes, from faux marquetry to marble tiles, from limed effects to the geometric checks we chose here. Paint can hide a multitude of sins and it is reassuring to know that floor varnishes today are so tough and hard-wearing that any paints used, no matter how delicate or thin, will be well protected. However, a pristine finish is not the only finish, indeed fashion for the distressed look has reached floor level and a little fading here or a scuff there is definitely now quite a coveted look, and one that will add immediate character to a room.

For wooden floors a thick coat of paint can unify battered boards while transparent effects will need some preparation in the form of filling and sanding. The price of a sanding machine and a few tools is really quite favourable compared to the cost of laying new boards or covering over completely with carpet.

If you worry that a hard, painted surface will be too noisy then a few brightly coloured rugs will add just the right amount of comfort. Do not forget that paint can be used to decorate the softer flooring materials such as sisal matting, or, better still, cheap cotton duck canvas, to make extremely decorative and versatile floor cloths.

If you are going for a painted finish, a thorough reading of the preparation requirements in Chapter 7 is strongly advised. In terms of materials most paint types can be used successfully. Latex (emulsion) paints are a little less resistant than the

A wash of transparent Slate Green was used over a solid coat of Smoke woodwash to create these large checks. These colours reflected the tones of the other paint effects and furnishings (left).

The sitting room floor boards were in remarkably good condition. All they needed was a sweep and a good scrub before a coat of latex (emulsion) was applied as a primer.

traditional oil-based paints used in earlier times but they dry very quickly and when applied over an acrylic primer and sealed with a good, acrylic varnish will make a perfectly adequate surface for further decoration, or simply left as a flat colour.

Checks are a very quick way of unifying an old floor that may be a little worse for wear, and they distract the eye from any damaged areas. They provide an opportunity for introducing pattern and colour into the interior within the safe confines of geometric order. Do not be put off by any irregularities in the shape or angles of your room as a dark border will absorb these and the pattern of the checks disguise them further.

When deciding on the size of your checks, remember that small checks can be busy, especially in bright colours, while large ones may look out of proportion in a small room. We chose a rather generous 30 in (75 cm) square as our room was relatively large. The checks can be drawn using a long ruler or, better still, a template around which they can be traced. Templates can be cut at very little expense from a piece of hardboard. Whichever size you choose remember to measure the length and width of the room and ensure the check divides equally into it to prevent broken shapes at either end of the room. Also make a note of the direction in which you enter the room as it may be more interesting to the eye to have the checks pointing out from the line of the wall, at an angle of 45 degrees, rather than running parallel to it. Black and white checks make a bold statement for entrance halls but their sharp contrast can be a little too hard for rooms used for relaxation. We used the alternate colours of slate green and smoke, the green being applied as a transparent wash of colour over the solid smoke background. These colours contributed just the right amount of colour to the room and echoed the tones of the other paint effects and furnishings.

wide decorator's brush

paint tray

Smoke Woodwash, or flat latex (matt emulsion) paint

pencil

30 × 30 in (75 × 75 cm) square of hardboard, or to fit dimensions of your room

low-tack masking tape

Slate Woodwash, or flat latex (matt emulsion) paint, diluted 2 parts water: 1 part paint

flat (matt) acrylic floor varnish paint brush

wide dragging brush

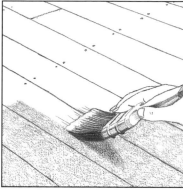

STEP 1 Prepare the floorboards as necessary and fill any holes as required. Using a wide decorator's brush, apply a solid coat of flat latex (matt emulsion) in a cream colour or Smoke Woodwash.

STEP 2 Starting in one corner, trace around the hardboard square, drawing in the checks lightly with pencil.

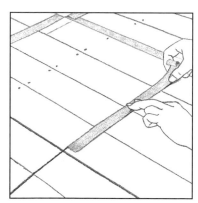

STEP 3 Mask off alternate squares using low-tack masking tape, making sure the corners of each check are sharp and that they meet precisely. Press the tape firmly to ensure that no paint bleeds underneath.

STEP 4 Using a wide dragging brush, apply the second colour to the alternate checks. Hold the brush almost flat against the floor surface and work in even strokes. Leave the floor to dry, then apply 2 coats of flat (matt) acrylic floor varnish.

JOCASTA'S TIP

An old LP record album sleeve makes the perfect ready-made template for creating smaller squares for this design.

Crackle-glazed table

For those who like the look of old paintwork but who are after a more contemporary feel, crackle glaze is the answer. While the craquelure technique utilizes the reaction between two transparent varnishes to create fine, porcelain fractures over an existing paint surface, crackle glaze is a thick, sticky medium which causes the paint itself to split, producing "alligator-skin" crazing. Sandwiched between two contrasting colours crackle glaze will produce an extremely dramatic effect with one colour peeping through the other.

Crackle glaze, which can be applied to any surface as long as it has been appropriately primed, is activated by water and so latex (emulsion) paint must be used with it. As soon as the top coat of paint touches the dried crackle glaze the reaction is instant: the paint splits and shrinks, revealing the colour beneath. The thicker the top coat of paint, the more dramatic the cracks, and these can be accentuated further by drying the area with a hairdrier. It is important to note that the direction of the cracks can be controlled as they follow the direction of the brushstrokes. Haphazard brushstrokes of both crackle glaze and the top coat will guarantee an interesting effect while horizontal and vertical strokes will be more regular.

As the reaction is immediate, care must be taken not to brush over the same area more than once otherwise the process will be interrupted. It is always a good idea to have a practice run first to get a feel of how much paint to take up on the brush and how quickly to move across the surface.

All sorts of colour combinations can be used. For a really stunning effect try black crackled over gold. To imitate leather try a dark brown over a lighter shade of the same colour, or, for a more gentle, sun-blistered look, try soft white over pale blue

We thought this well-made but slightly damaged coffee table would benefit from some rich and sophisticated colour (left).

Dark green "crackled" on rich red. Crackle glaze causes one water-based colour to crack and split over another, producing a dramatic, alligator-skin effect (right).

JOCASTA'S TIP

For a more naturally crackled look, try applying the crackle glaze only to the areas that would become scuffed with time; this way the paint will only crack in certain places.

MATERIALS AND EQUIPMENT

medium-grade
sandpaper

dusting brush

Barn Red and Slate
Woodwash, or flat
latex (matt
emulsion) paint

paint brushes

crackle glaze

hairdrier (optional)

oil-based varnish

rich brown boot
polish (optional)

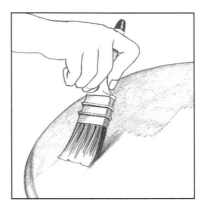

STEP 1 Lightly sand the table
with medium-grade sandpaper.
Dust down and apply a solid coat
of the Barn Red Woodwash or
latex (emulsion). Leave to dry
thoroughly.

STEP 2 Apply a coat of crackle
glaze using a clean brush. Take
care to spread the glaze evenly;
dampening the brush in water can
help with this. As you brush, alter
the direction of the brush strokes
to ensure a dramatic effect.

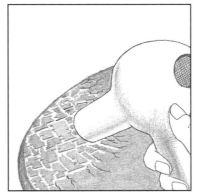

STEP 3 Apply a coat of Slate
Woodwash, or latex (emulsion),
again altering the direction of the
brush strokes. Work quickly,
making sure you do not go back
and forth over the same areas. If
you like, use a hairdrier on a hot
setting to accelerate the drying and
exaggerate the cracked effect.
Leave to dry and finish cracking.

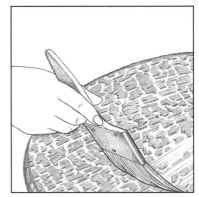

STEP 4 Apply a thick coat of oil-
based varnish. A flat (matt) varnish
is more natural but, for a slight
gleam, polish the surface afterwards with a rich brown boot
polish.

Crackle glaze is suitable for many different surfaces – wood, metal and plastic – and can transform an object before your eyes in minutes.

or yellow. For the most subtle effect of all try white on white. If you want to achieve a more genuinely antique look then try dragging over a wash of raw umber which will settle in the cracks imitating the build-up of grime. The raw umber would have to be oil-based so as not to re-activate the glaze.

Whichever colour combination you use, crackle glaze must be one of the most satisfying paint techniques as it happens literally before your eyes and can be great fun to try with children. One word of warning: always remember to seal your final effect with an oil-based varnish or you may risk the whole lot washing off.

Découpage fire screen

Découpage, which literally means "cutting out", is the perfect technique for those who are not so confident of their free-hand painting skills. This paper craft, which involves the application of cut-out images to a surface which is then covered in layers of varnish or lacquer, can look as sophisticated and elegant or as naïve as you wish. In the eighteenth century the craft became extraordinarily popular. In Europe, particularly in Italy, the demand for hand-painted furniture far outstripped supply and furniture pattern books were printed by the thousand and motifs cut directly from them. Although it was known as "poor man's" art, it quickly became a respected art form in itself giving rise to star practitioners, such as Mrs Delaney in Britain. The aim of découpage was to trick the eye into believing the piece had been painstakingly hand painted at great expense. Ladies of the day took it up as a pastime and decorative arts museums across the world have many exquisite examples of screens and boxes, cabinets and desks embellished in hand-coloured, tissue-thin flowers and cherubs, architectural motifs or chinoiserie.

In Victorian times the technique was just as popular but the style was a little more relaxed. Ready-coloured "scraps" were used in a more haphazard way, emphasizing the richness and humour of a particular collection of images rather than the correct perspective and immaculate finish of the painted style.

Sources for découpage motifs are numerous. For ready-coloured motifs, wrapping paper, magazine cut-outs or even pieces of wallpaper can be used. For those who want to create their own colour schemes, photocopies can be made from books of old engravings or manuscripts and then hand coloured using water colour paints. A craquelure (cracked) varnish is certainly not obligatory but it is often used as the final stage to give an "antique" finish.

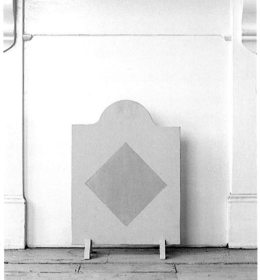

We needed a decorative fire screen to distract the eye from the boarded-up grate and create an eye-catching and elegant ornament (above).

Here photocopies were taken from an architectural print book to create a design. A craquelure finish, the fine crazing of varnish, was applied over the top (right).

MATERIALS AND EQUIPMENT

medium-grade sandpaper

dusting brush

white acrylic satin (eggshell) paint

paint brushes

repeated photocopied images

scissors

white polish shellac

wallpaper paste

Two-part Craquelure Varnish (or an oil-based varnish and a water-based varnish)

raw umber artist's oil paint

soft rag

mid-sheen (eggshell) oil-based varnish

For our découpage fire screen we used a collection of architectural prints to create a design. The linear quality of the prints is emphasized, together with a clever play on perspective. The raw umber oil paint rubbed into the craquelure cracks provides just the right antique tint to knock back the whiteness of the prints. Using a single large print cuts down the time needed for cutting out; large paper motifs can be stuck to any surface, including large pieces of furniture and walls. Prints applied directly to walls are excellent for decorating a room quickly and economically, creating a very elegant interior.

The techniques for découpage have relaxed greatly over the years, but for those who want a very smooth finish several coats of an acrylic gesso are recommended at the preparation stage, followed by several coats of quick-drying acrylic varnish to seal the motifs. Some professionals apply as many as 40 coats of varnish, sanding in between, but for the busy decorator the technique shown here may be more appropriate.

Découpage can be applied to almost any item of furniture or accessory.

STEP 1 Sand the firescreen lightly using medium-grade sandpaper. Dust down and apply a coat of white acrylic satin (eggshell) paint. As the paint is thick, use strong regular strokes when brushing it on.

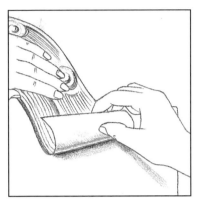

STEP 2 Trim the photocopies if necessary to fit the area of the screen you are going to decorate. Seal the images with a coat of white polish shellac to stiffen them. Leave to dry. Cut out carefully and stick onto the screen using wallpaper paste. Once the design is complete apply another coat of white polish shellac to seal the surface.

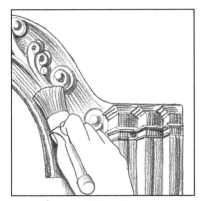

STEP 3 Apply Two-Part Craquelure Varnish, spreading it evenly over the surface of the screen. If you are not using a proprietary craquelure varnish, use a coat of the oil-based varnish and then apply a coat of water-based varnish.

JOCASTA'S TIP

Try dusting gold or silver powders over the craquelure with a soft mop head brush to create fine, delicate, cobweb-like cracks.

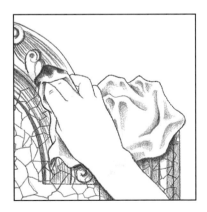

STEP 4 Leave the varnish until dry by which time the cracks will have appeared. Rub artist's oil paint into the cracks using a soft rag. Only use artist's oil paint because it dries very slowly, allowing any excess paint to be rubbed off once the cracks have been filled. Seal with a coat of white polish shellac and leave to dry. Apply a coat of mid-sheen (eggshell) varnish to finish off.

THE KITCHEN

*U*NLIKE THE SITTING room, the kitchen posed a few problems, although these were easily rectified once work started. The chief difficulty was the narrowness and height of the room, which lacked any other focal point to distract the eye. These upward lines were accentuated by a rather eccentric and dominating 1940s kitchen cupboard, left by the last tenants. Its vertical aspect did nothing to soften the uncomfortable shape of the room. Also, there was the rather incongruous mixture of 1970s chrome-edged laminate cabinets, which, like the rest of the room – apart from the brown carpet – were a cold, hard white. What we needed were some tricks to divert the eye from these awkward features, and some good strong colours to add warmth and a sense of unity.

A problematic room, too narrow, too tall with mismatched furniture, but soon to be transformed by our decorative scheme.

Colour was seen as the most important element for renovating this kitchen. Bold, primary colour for the walls and eccentric cupboard, and stencilling in blues and reds for the floor helped to distract the eye from the odd proportions of the room (right).

Impasto walls

The use of high-build paints to create textured wall surfaces is often overlooked as a decorating option because of associations with the rather mesmerizing, swirly, knobbly or prickly effects of the 1960s and 1970s. However, these are not the only looks to be achieved and increasingly decorators are using these paints to imitate the more romantic effects of rustic country walls or rough plastering.

Textured finishes are available either in powder form or ready mixed, and their great advantage is that any number of imperfections, cracks or bumps can be concealed, as well as unsightly and out-dated wall coverings such as woodchip paper, textured wallpaper or prickly textured coating. The thick, creamy consistency of my Impasto paint will smooth these away in just one coat and then almost obliterate them with the application of further coats.

Quite a range of effects can be achieved and textured finishes should by no means be seen simply as a solution to problem walls. Even if you have pristine, newly plastered walls, one soft coat of a watered-down textured paint can give a gentle and more homely feel to your interior. Applied in a cross-hatching motion with a wide, stiff-bristled decorator's brush the effect can be very similar to traditional distemper. Used neat from the pot and applied thickly, a very animated surface can be achieved which can then be sanded back after colour has been applied to create a distressed look. It will take time and quite a lot of energy but it will produce a very satisfying finish for those who want to indulge their imagination a little and be transported from the normal associations of their domestic interior. As most of these paints come untinted it is only when colour is applied that the full effect of the finish can be appreciated and the texture is completely visible. It is possible to stain a textured paint beforehand using acrylics, universal stainers or water-borne powder pigments but difficulties can arise in the distribution of the colour as the material is dense and a lot of tint is needed. It is probably easier to cover over the

Impasto effect for walls: thick textured paint is brushed on roughly with a coarse bristle brush and given a coat of latex (emulsion) before being sanded back to create a rustic, crumbling effect.

JOCASTA'S TIP

For a very animated surface apply the textured paint with a trowel.

MATERIALS AND EQUIPMENT

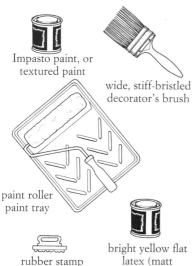

Impasto paint, or textured paint

wide, stiff-bristled decorator's brush

paint roller
paint tray

rubber stamp

bright yellow flat latex (matt emulsion) paint

dark blue flat latex (matt emulsion) paint

tiny paint roller

old newspaper

coarse-grade sandpaper

sanding block

STEP 1 Prepare the walls as necessary. Apply the textured paint using a wide decorator's brush and brushing in thick, cross-hatching strokes to build up a rough surface. Leave to dry.

STEP 2 Using a roller, apply a coat of bright yellow flat latex (matt emulsion) to the dry textured paint. Do not worry if the textured surface does not pick up the colour completely as this will add to the final distressed look.

STEP 3 Evenly coat the rubber stamp with a layer of dark blue flat latex (matt emulsion) paint using a tiny roller. Blot the stamp on old newspaper before applying it to the wall to remove any excess paint and to test the image. Work out the position of each stamped motif carefully before pressing it firmly against the wall.

STEP 4 When the stamp design is complete, leave to dry. Next, vigorously rub back each wall using coarse-grade sandpaper wrapped around a sanding block. This will expose the textured surface beneath the yellow paint in any raised areas, producing a rustic finish.

An impasto wall which has been colourwashed and then stencilled with a repeated motif. Impasto is ideal for disguising damaged or cracked walls.

paint after it has been applied to the wall. You can use either a coat of latex (emulsion) if a flat, chalky finish is desired, or a colourwash if you want a more transparent finish. Once sanded back using medium-grade sandpaper over a block both of these effects will look astonishingly like ancient walls and can be embellished further with rustic stamps or stencils. For our colourful kitchen we chose a thick, flat (matt), bright yellow emulsion stamped to chair (dado) rail height with a blue tile motif. After being sanded, both colours took on a wonderfully faded appearance as though they had been gently bleached by the warm rays of the sun somewhere in deepest Spain.

Faux panelling

Plastic laminates on chipboard and blockboard when first introduced were very popular in kitchens and bathrooms as they were more easily cleaned, looked "modern" and were extremely efficient at resisting moisture and heat. The fashion, however, has turned again and many people are replacing their white laminate or imitation wood finishes with hand-built, painted units.

What about those who cannot afford to replace an entire kitchen scheme, or indeed feel it is extravagant to rip out a perfectly efficient scheme just in the name of fashion? Well, the answer, once again, is paint. If these surfaces are properly prepared and sealed after decorating, more or less any effect can be achieved. For our white kitchen cabinets we washed and sanded the door fronts before priming them in two coats of water-based acrylic primer. This is very useful for painting over existing paint or varnishing layers without stripping.

We employed a simple *trompe-l'œil* effect to show how the flush doors could be broken up and given the impression of a recessed panel using monochrome glazes. We chose shades of blue for our glaze work to reflect the colour in the rest of the room, the floor painting and the eccentric kitchen cupboard.

When measuring the door to create the panel a good sense of proportion is crucial as borders that are too narrow or wide will look unbalanced. If in doubt as to proportion, look at existing moulding elsewhere in the house. Also, an appreciation of the way light falls on surfaces and creates shadow is very important. Some skilled professionals are able to create the illusion of elaborate mouldings with undulations of multiple recesses and beading. Here we have stuck to a very simple system of light and dark with two sides of the panel (top and left-hand side) in the lighter shade and the other two sides (bottom and right-hand side) in the darker shade.

MATERIALS AND EQUIPMENT

strong detergent

scouring pad

silicon carbide (wet-and-dry) paper

dusting brush

acrylic primer

protractor

paint brushes, including two 3 in (75 mm) brushes and a fitch

low-tack masking tape

pencil

artist's acrylic paints in ultramarine, raw umber and white

acrylic scumble glaze

water

flat (matt) acrylic varnish

satin latex (vinyl silk) emulsion paint

Painted kitch

Having ripped up the very ugly and unh
had discovered floor boards that were
condition. These were painted using Smoke
furniture paint to unify and neaten the floor
more light to the room, but some sort of des
was needed to guide the eye downwards to t
area, away from the vertical lines of the narr

Stencilling is an ideal way of creating a f
ready-made template that can be repeated ov
the process relatively quick; time is a key fac
activity must cease until the floor is finished
the shape of the room is broken up with per
cabinets or other pieces of furniture, a centr
such as the rug painted here is easier to exec
all-over design.

The floor surface needs to be relatively s
stencilling if the design is going to look crisp
and splits can be filled and sanded beforeha
for floor preparation). We used a ready-mad
could hand-cut your own by looking at a cla
copying the motifs, tracing them onto stenci
cutting them out carefully using a sharp craf
Technically, floors are stencilled in the same
the key factor is to remember to use very litt
the brush on newspaper before
applying the design; this
prevents the paint from bleeding
beneath the stencil and
smudging the motif. The stencil
brush should be dome-ended as
this will help in shading colours;
the paints should be water-based
as they will dry more or less
immediately and allow for a
second colour to be applied.

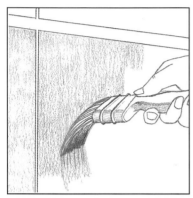 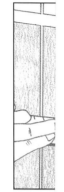  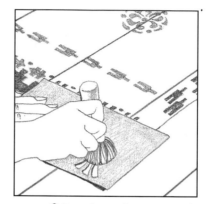 

STEP 1 Scrub down the laminated surfaces of the kitchen cabinets with a strong detergent and scouring pad to ensure that all grease and grime are removed. Sand each surface thoroughly using silicon carbide (wet-and-dry) paper. Dust down and prime with one coat of acrylic primer. Leave to dry.

STEP 2 the pane... with a s... latex (vi... paint is ... the glaze... too quic... for the g... to dry, t... (7.5 cm)... each cor... 45 degre...

STEP 1 To emphasize the rug area against the dark-painted floor boards, paint an opaque rectangle to the size required in a base colour of cream flat latex (matt emulsion). Leave to dry. Remember not to position the "rug" too close to the kitchen furniture, especially if your kitchen is small, as it may create a cluttered look.

STEP 2 Decide on the pattern of the stencilled motifs and attach the first stencil to the floor using low-tack masking tape. Stipple in the design using artist's acrylic paints and varying sizes of stencilling brush. Take care not to overload the brushes with paint – only very small amounts are needed. Continue stencilling until the rug pattern is complete. Leave the paint to dry.

STEP 3 Drag a wash of the diluted red latex (matt emulsion) paint over the design using a wide varnish brush. This helps to soften the design and gives the rug the appearance of being more substantial. Add a little more red paint to the wash and paint a darker border around the edge of the rug area to contain the design. Leave to dry.

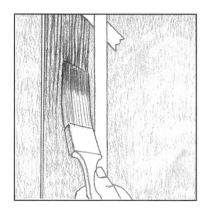   

STEP 4 to drag ... masked ... almost f... best to ... so as to ... shades ... shade to ... borders ... right-ha... When th... masking... of flat (... allowing... before a...

JOCASTA'S TIP

To achieve an aged appearance for the newly painted floor, tint the acrylic floor varnish with a little burnt umber artist's paint.

STEP 4 Using medium-grade sandpaper, lightly sand back the paintwork to create a softly distressed look. Dust down. Protect the rug by applying two coats of acrylic floor varnish, allowing the first coat to dry before applying the second. This varnish will not yellow with time, so the colours of the rug should remain bright.

Distressed chair

For centuries craftsmen have scratched and bashed, rubbed and dabbed to give character and history to their newly decorated pieces. Though some today may find it perverse to abrade or virtually obliterate fresh paint effects, there is no doubt that a wash of raw umber or a quick rub with wire wool adds intrigue and subtlety to colour and texture.

The popularity of the "distressed look" stems from the idea that old equals desirable. Although this may upset those designers who would prefer to celebrate the sleeker and more pristine qualities of chrome, glass, steel and plastics, for the average homeowner there are some advantages in choosing a distressed finish. Apart from adding immediate romance to what could otherwise be an insignificant piece, distressing can disguise inferior surface materials such as plywood, laminates or cheap pine. Unfortunately, not all of us are lucky enough to afford or inherit true antiques but, with a few clever tricks, you can add just the right touch of friendly decrepitude to your interior, creating intimacy and character. Such blatant artifice can be forgiven, especially in the light of the increasing impersonality that has come with the computer age and all its technological developments. After all, artifice is very much what paint effects are all about. So if you've got it, flaunt it; if you haven't, fake it!

Some craftsmen employ such extreme tools as blow torches, paint stripper or even chains, but very effective distressing can be achieved through the less harsh means of washes, waxes and wire wools. Before you start look hard at a naturally aged piece to see how time has eroded the paintwork and how the grime has built up. It is in the most prominent areas where the paintwork has worn away – the outward curve of a turned leg, the crest of the mouldings, door handles, sharp corners – and the recesses and grooves where the residue of time has collected. Distressing can look unconvincing if done half-heartedly or, worse, done in inappropriate areas.

Distressing is the perfect finishing touch for an old kitchen chair. A wax candle rubbed here and there acts as a barrier between two different coloured water-based-paints.

Before its transformation our kitchen chair needed a new seat which was cut from a sheet of hardboard using a jigsaw.

MATERIALS AND EQUIPMENT

medium-grade sandpaper (optional)

acrylic primer (optional)

Conifer Green Woodwash or flat latex (matt emulsion) paint

paint brushes

household candle

Barn Red Woodwash or flat latex (matt emulsion) paint

coarse wire wool

rich brown boot polish (optional)

New, cheap pine frames can look a lot more interesting with a distressed paint effect. These frames have been embellished further with stencils which have also been gently rubbed back to make them blend with the rest of the effect.

For an extremely quick form of distressing, medium-grade sandpaper or wire wool can be used simply to rub back existing paintwork here and there. Another method is to mix a wash of raw umber acrylic colour and drag over your paintwork before varnishing. Alternatively, tint the varnish itself. For a heavily encrusted look, add brown or grey powder pigment to beeswax and brush it on so that it settles in the mouldings of the piece; leave to harden and then buff it back to give a gentle shine. If you want a more colourful look, follow the two-colour heavy-distressing technique shown here; it involves an intriguing combination of colours, antiquing waxes and a household candle. This method is particularly suitable for rustic pieces of furniture and makes a very good background for later applications of stencilled designs.

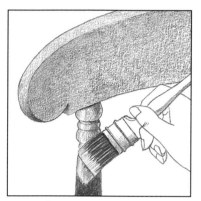  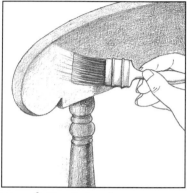

STEP 1 Prepare the woodwork on the chair (if it has previously been painted with gloss paint, sand it thoroughly and apply a coat of acrylic primer). Paint the chair with a solid coat of the dark green flat latex (matt emulsion), taking care not to miss the undersides of the chair and any recesses. Leave to dry.

STEP 2 Rub the candle onto the areas of the chair which would normally receive the most wear and tear. To create strong gashes and streaks, press hard with the end of the candle; for a speckled effect rub the whole length of the candle over the surface.

STEP 3 Gently brush away any large crumbs of wax and then apply a coat of red latex (matt emulsion) paint. The wax acts as a barrier between the two colours, preventing the red from adhering to the green. Leave the paint to dry thoroughly.

JOCASTA'S TIP

If you want a lot of the bottom colour to show through the top colour, begin rubbing the top colour away with the wire wool before it has dried completely. The wire wool will become very sticky but the look is dramatic.

STEP 4 Rub the paintwork all over using coarse wire wool, following the direction of the woodwork. The top coat will slowly rub away in the areas where the wax was applied to reveal the paint beneath. At the same time the rubbing action gives the paint a burnished look that can be enriched further with rich brown boot polish, if desired.

THE BATHROOM

THOUGH GENEROUSLY PROPORTIONED, which is unusual for bathrooms, this room was probably the bleakest of all. On our arrival we were confronted by a veritable lattice-work of exposed copper piping, a floor covered in old, ripped linoleum, walls painted in institution-green and a window screened only by a grubby net curtain. However, these were superficial problems and, as every decorator knows, it is often the grimmest of rooms that are the easiest and most satisfying to tackle. We had great fun introducing hot, earthy colours and a few glittering special effects that brought about a radical and truly exotic transformation.

The bathroom looked particularly grim before its transformation – ripped lino, a tangle of pipes and institution-green walls.

Creating warmth was the priority in the bathroom. A rich terracotta colourwash did this quickly. An exotic element was then introduced with a mosaic stamp effect and gold leaf details (far right).

Mosaic stamp effect

Stamps are a wonderfully quick and effective way of decorating walls, floors, furniture and fabric. Once a design has been cut it can be repeated over and over with great ease using quick-drying latex (emulsion) or acrylic colours. The variation caused by the differing thicknesses of the stamped paint emphasizes the naïve, hand-printed look.

Stamps can be cut out of rubber (some companies will produce a stamp to your own design), a potato, or a synthetic household sponge. Here, to complement the exotic theme of the bathroom, we modelled little cubes out of a synthetic sponge to imitate a mosaic effect. The walls were colourwashed beforehand to create a deep terracotta background on top of which a border was ruled at chair (dado) rail height. Cream-coloured latex (emulsion) paint was used to produce the gently stamped blocks of mosaic cubes below this rail level and then individual cubes were stamped on in midnight blue and gold.

It is always a good idea to blot the stamp on some old newspaper after it has been pressed face-down in the wet paint, but any smears or smudges can also be gently wiped away with a damp rag or another sponge. While the holes in the sponge material itself will guarantee variety in the stamped look, you should aim for clean, crisp edges or the clarity of the design will be lost. The gold mosaic pieces were made by covering some of the emulsioned cubes with gilding size (glue) and pressing on Dutch metal leaf (see p.163 for full instructions) to create a truly glittering effect. It is always best to seal any effects where water may be splashed; here we used an oil-based varnish.

Synthetic sponges are ideal for creating decorative stamps for walls, furniture or fabrics. The honeycomb formation of the sponge guarantees variety in the stamped finish.

MATERIALS AND EQUIPMENT

Deep Terracotta Colourwash, or other colourwash paint

tape measure

spirit level

large, rectangular, synthetic household sponge

paint brushes, including a fine water colour brush

pencil

black felt-tip pen

craft knife

flat latex (matt emulsion) paint in various colours, including cream

paint tray

old newspapers

water-based gilding size

Dutch metal leaf in sheets

acrylic varnish

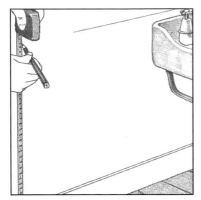

STEP 1 Prepare the walls and colourwash them a deep terracotta shade. Using a tape measure, pencil and spirit level, mark in a chair (dado) rail around the room (this rail is usually 3 ft [90 cm] from the floor).

STEP 2 Using a black felt-tip pen, draw channels ¼ in (6 mm) thick to divide 1 in (2.5 cm) squares on a synthetic household sponge. Carefully hollow out the channels using a craft knife. The raised square areas will produce the "mosaic" shapes.

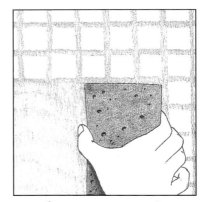

STEP 3 Pour some cream flat latex (matt emulsion) paint into a paint tray and lightly press the face of the sponge into it. Blot the sponge on some old newspapers to make sure that all the squares are covered in paint. Stamp the sponge onto the walls in regular blocks until the wall surface is covered from chair (dado) rail to baseboard (skirting board). Remember to reload the sponge with paint as often as necessary. When finished, leave the squares to dry.

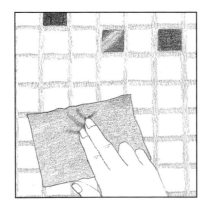

STEP 4 Cut a single square from the sponge and stamp on individual colours to create a border. Using a fine water colour brush, paint over some of the white squares with water-based gilding size. Wait for this to become "tacky" (sticky but not wet) and then press on single sheets of Dutch metal leaf. Peel away the backing paper and brush away any excess metal leaf. Once the effect is complete, seal each wall with acrylic varnish.

JOCASTA'S TIP

To achieve a stronger glittery look, add tiny mirror squares (often found in tile shops) here and there or alternatively in straight rows for a truly sparkling impression.

Rust-effect bathroom chair

The craze for imitation metal effects on decorative objects has progressed from the very popular verdigris finish to new ones such as rust. Some may think it eccentric to actually go out of one's way to create this finish but the soft reddish bloom of the rust colour really does give a rich yet subtle patina to the crudest of objects.

Genuine rust is, of course, created by the exposure of metal to the elements and it is the mimicry of the soft, dry, powdery state of the corroded metal that is the key to this technique, as well as achieving the appropriate colour. There are corrosive materials available on the market that will produce this effect by attacking the metal itself but these can be dangerous and unpleasant to use. The safest and most satisfying way of creating a rust effect is to apply flat latex (matt emulsion) or acrylic colours in a soft, stippling action onto a base colour. For the base colour we used a dark blue-black in a thick opaque coat, followed by two stippled colours of dark red and then orange to create the vivid, gritty highlights that are quite astonishingly bright if you look closely at a genuinely rusted piece. All metal objects are suitable and can be treated immediately if the object has been cleaned, sanded and primed in red oxide metal primer first. Candlesticks, wrought-iron balustrades and light fixtures are just some of the objects that could be transformed. Plastic and wood can also be treated if primed appropriately.

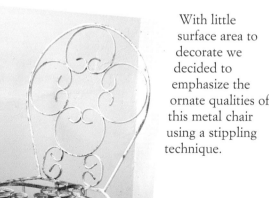

With little surface area to decorate we decided to emphasize the ornate qualities of this metal chair using a stippling technique.

MATERIALS AND EQUIPMENT

wire brush

metal primer, for example red oxide

paint brushes, including a 1 in (25 mm) brush

round-ended stencilling brush

Rust Kit, or artist's acrylic paints in assorted colours

old newspapers

flat (matt) oil-based varnish

Rich red and vivid orange are stippled onto a dark blue-black background to imitate the subtle patina of ancient rust. Metallic waxes can be applied here and there to create glittering highlights (left).

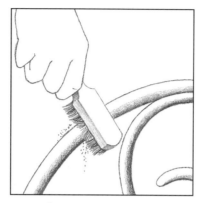

STEP 1 Brush down the old metal work using a tough wire brush to clear away any dust or loose particles. Prime the metal chair surface with a special metal primer, such as red oxide, and leave to dry.

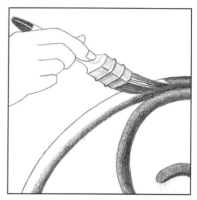

STEP 2 If mixing your own paint colours, prepare the base coat by mixing a dark blue-black colour using artist's acrylic paints, and paint it on as a solid coat. For ornate and intricate areas use a 1 in (25 mm) brush. Leave to dry.

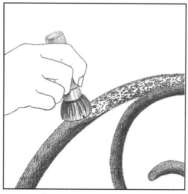

STEP 3 For the first stippling colour, mix a dark, rich red, and for the second, a bright acid orange. Stipple these colours onto the chair using the tip of a round-ended stencilling brush. Use a tiny amount of paint at a time and work it through the bristles of the brush on some newspaper so that the brush is almost dry.

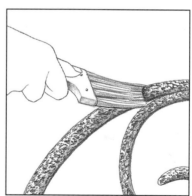

STEP 4 Stipple more of the orange colour onto prominent areas of the piece. Leave to dry. Finish off by applying a coat of flat (matt) oil-based varnish.

Frosted window pane

Painting on glass belongs to an old tradition and one of the prettiest ways of achieving privacy for an interior without having to resort to the usual fabric coverings that cut out a lot of light. Coloured glass paints can be used to imitate stained-glass effects and materials are now available which imitate the lead framework in which the stained-glass pieces are set.

Water-based paste solutions can also be used to imitate the snowy translucency of frosted or etched glass and produce an incredibly delicate and beautiful screen for the lower panels of windows. We used a solution of wallpaper paste, PVA glue and white powder paint, stippled through a stencil directly onto the glass to create a design. We designed a border to create a strong frame which contained a spray of different-sized stars.

Care has to be taken not to smudge the design while it is still wet but the beauty is that all paints can be scraped off the glass with a razor blade or wire wool if you get into difficulties. Edges can be neatened and motifs more clearly defined after they have dried. To seal the effect there are industrial xioline-based glazes that adhere well to glass and which are extremely durable, but these may be difficult to find. Polyurethane varnish, applied with a brush, will create ripples which resemble the imperfections in old glass though the effect will yellow a little with time. Best of all would be a synthetic acrylic aerosol spray varnish which will provide a fine, water-resistant coating with little mess or washing up afterwards.

If you are really patient you can work in reverse order and stipple the entire pane, allow it to dry and then etch a design into it. Where the paste is worked away the light will shine through. The paste is so soft that you will not need to use a very sharp tool, which may graze the glass.

All these effects could also be applied to mirror glass, to glass-topped furniture or to glass-panelled doors. If you want a slight tint then add a tiny drop of diluted acrylic colour or water-borne powder pigment to create a soft, powdery, frosted colour to match your wall colour or furnishings.

MATERIALS AND EQUIPMENT

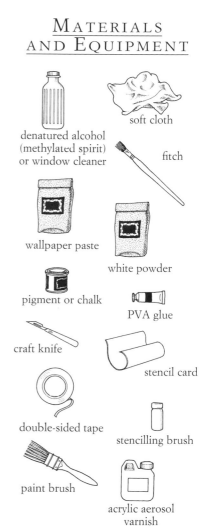

denatured alcohol
(methylated spirit)
or window cleaner

soft cloth

fitch

wallpaper paste

white powder

pigment or chalk

PVA glue

craft knife

stencil card

double-sided tape

stencilling brush

paint brush

acrylic aerosol
varnish

A frosted glass effect created with wallpaper paste provides privacy for the bathroom.

STEP 1 Wash down the glass with denatured alcohol (methylated spirit) and a soft cloth, or with a proprietary window cleaner, to remove any grease and grime.

STEP 2 Using a fitch, mix up half a cup of wallpaper paste following the manufacturer's instructions. Make the paste whiter and more opaque by adding a little white powder pigment or chalk until it resembles half-melted snow in colour. Add a drop of PVA glue to bind the ingredients.

STEP 3 Using a craft knife and stencil card, cut out stencils for two different star shapes. Attach the stencils to the glass in the required position using small pieces of double-sided tape on the back of each star. Stencil around each shape using a stencilling brush dipped in a small amount of wallpaper paste solution. Use gentle, stippling strokes. When dry, remove the templates.

STEP 4 Although the solution will set hard, it is wise to protect the design with a varnish. Spray on a light coat of acrylic aerosol varnish from a distance of 18 in (45 cm). If you have difficulty finding this varnish, some companies that produce glass paints also offer complementary varnishes.

A rather more elaborate affair – a cut-out design is stuck temporarily to the window pane using spray adhesive and the frosting solution stippled around it (right).

JOCASTA'S TIP

To create an attractive border around a solid pane of frosting, apply a thin strip of lining tape a little way in from the edge of the glass and paint the whole pane with the solution. Remove the tape when the solution is completely dry.

Gilded striped frame

As you can see from the "before" shots, our rather glamorous mirror was produced from a very battered old frame found in the bathroom. It came with no glass or fixtures, only built-up grime and lots of cracks. Frames are one of the easiest and most satisfying objects on which to try your hand at a new technique. Their surface area is relatively small and so perfect for practising the more fiddly paint effects. They can usually be picked up at garage sales or markets at very little cost, relieving you of the worry of ruining any valuable items.

After filling the cracks with ready-mixed spackle (filler) and sanding down the frame, we chose a dramatic combination of a midnight blue base colour and striking gold-leaf stripes. This is not genuine gold leaf, but Dutch metal, the versatile, cheaper alternative that can be used in a variety of different ways. Increasingly, many gilders now use this material, not only because it is cheaper (about a third of the price) but because it really can be made to look impressive with the clever use of antiquing glazes and dry powders such as rotten stone. It is applied to the surface using either an oil- or water-based size (glue) which is left to become tacky before the Dutch metal is pressed on and any loose fragments gently brushed away. This material is much tougher than real gold leaf, and does not necessitate a gesso base as in traditional gilding, but it will tarnish and so must be sealed with a shellac or varnish. It comes either as loose leaves or backed by tissue sheets, and can be cut to size using sharp scissors to fit a certain shape. This will prevent wastage.

Coloured glazes can be applied over the top to create glamorous effects such as tortoiseshell or fantasy marbles, and stencilled patterns can be created by using the gold size as a stencilling medium before pressing on the Dutch metal and brushing away the excess leaf. At Christmas time it is great fun to gild walnuts in this way and antique them with a little boot polish to make decorative table or tree accessories.

This battered mirror frame needed some attention. It had to be filled, primed and thoroughly sanded before gilding could begin (above).

Gold and dark blue are always a handsome combination. Sheets of gold leaf known as Dutch metal are applied to the frame using water-based gilding size.

MATERIALS AND EQUIPMENT

fine silicon carbide
(wet-and-dry) paper

dusting brush

Midnight Blue
Woodwash or flat
latex (matt
emulsion) paint

paint brushes

low-tack masking
tape

pencil

tape measure

lining tape

1 in (25 mm)
varnish brush

Dutch gold metal
leaf in sheets

water-based gilding
size

soft wire wool

flat (matt) acrylic
varnish

With clever antiquing effects
Dutch metal can be made to
look truly stunning. Soft wire
wool is used to distress the leaf
on the prominent areas while
powders create a built-up patina
in the recesses.

STEP 1 Prepare the mirror frame as necessary. Sand down the woodwork with fine silicon carbide (wet-and-dry) paper. Dust down.

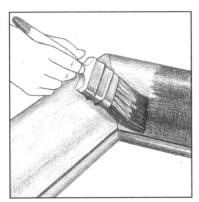

STEP 2 Paint the whole frame with two coats of dark blue flat latex (matt emulsion) paint, leaving the first coat to dry before applying the second. You may want to remove the glass temporarily from the frame, or else protect it with low-tack masking tape.

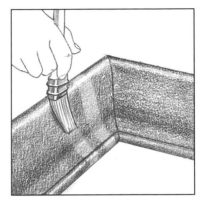

STEP 3 Using a pencil, lightly mark 3 in (7.5 cm) bands at regular intervals on the frame. Create thin lines dividing each band by laying down strips of very narrow lining tape to block off the area. Paint the bands with water-based gilding size using a 1 in (25 mm) varnish brush.

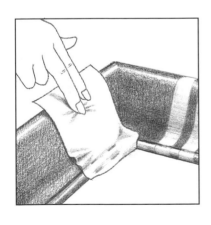

STEP 4 Leave the size for about 10 minutes until tacky. Take a sheet of Dutch metal leaf and press it onto the size. Rub the back of the transfer paper gently before peeling it off. Brush away any excess gold with a soft, dry brush. Once all the stripes are gilded, rub back slightly with soft wire wool to distress the gold a little. Remove the lining tape. Seal the frame with a flat (matt) acrylic varnish.

JOCASTA'S TIP

For an alternative method of applying Dutch metal leaf, paint on the size through a stencil to achieve different gilded shapes.

THE BEDROOM

BEDROOMS SHOULD BE comfortable and a pleasure to be in at all times, and we chose unabashedly soft and gentle shades to transform this one. That is not to say, however, that these are your run-of-the-mill pastels. Instead, they were based on traditional Scandinavian colour schemes – dusty blues and silvery greys combined with warm, buff tones. A dormer window made this room the most interesting of the four in terms of its shape, and the most challenging where the wall effect was concerned as it was difficult to decide where the wall ended and the ceiling began. We decided against carpeting over the floor boards but gave the wood a gentle, rustic feel using washes of water-based colour to bring out the grain.

A dormer window made this room particularly interesting. The floor boards were in good condition but the room definitely needed warm tones and some pretty details.

Stencilled "wallpaper"

The current vogue in stencilling techniques is the all-over wallpaper approach which incorporates bold, large-scale, repeated schemes. This trend has been heavily influenced by traditional Scandinavian paint effects, where stencilling became a useful alternative at times when labour was cheap and imported papers expensive. Wallpapers are still expensive, especially the high-quality ones, and the beauty of employing stencils in this method is that tracings can be made from historical or contemporary wallpaper sample books, transferred onto stencil card and cut by hand. Inevitably, there will be the odd smudge or wobble that will give the game away, but this will only add to the originality and subtleness of the scheme.

Photocopiers are a great help in enlarging or reducing your chosen motif. Other useful equipment to have at hand is a plumb line and level to achieve balanced and even spacing, as placement of the motifs is crucial. If too widely spaced, the design will lose its impact; if packed too closely, the effect will be fussy and a strain on the eye. It is important to look hard at a room that has been papered and note how the shape of the walls has affected the papered design. Your spacing should not be interrupted by door or window frames, by sloping ceilings or built-in fixtures but should continue regardless. If your column of motifs ends up falling in a tricky corner, or is sliced through by a slanting attic window, the motifs must continue regardless or they will unbalance the design.

A particularly subtle paint effect can be achieved by stencilling in acrylics over a distressed background such as the colourwash here. Afterwards you can lightly sand back the motifs to distress them even further, creating gently faded colours. Although there are many companies that offer ranges of pre-cut stencils you can have fun cutting your own. Stencil card, which is treated with linseed oil to protect it from the moisture of paint, is readily available from most craft stores. Having traced your design onto the card, using either transfer or carbon paper, cut the shapes using a good-quality, sharp craft knife.

MATERIALS AND EQUIPMENT

cream satin latex (vinyl silk emulsion) paint

paint roller
paint tray

Buff Colourwash, or other colourwash paint

softening brush

tracing paper

motif

pencil

stencil card

carbon paper

craft knife

Swedish Blue Colourwash, or artist's acrylic paints in cerulean blue, white and raw umber

low-tack masking tape

stencilling brush

An economical and original "wallpaper" can be produced by stencilling onto a colourwash ground.

STEP 1 Prepare the walls and then paint them with a coat of cream satin latex (vinyl silk emulsion) using a roller. Leave to dry, then apply a coat of Buff colourwash using a softening brush to create a slightly more animated effect.

STEP 2 Choose your preferred stencil motif and trace it onto tracing paper. Then transfer it to stencil card using carbon paper.

STEP 3 Place the stencil card on a flat, hard protected surface, preferably a cutting board, and cut out the motif with a craft knife. Position the blade at an angle to create a bevelled edge; this will help prevent the paint bleeding beneath the edges.

JOCASTA'S TIP

If the surface of the wall is very delicate, use low-tack spray adhesive instead of masking tape, but be sure to work in a well-ventilated area and avoid inhaling the vapours.

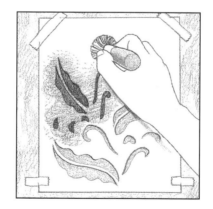

STEP 4 If you are mixing your own blue paint for stencilling, use artist's acrylic paints and combine cerulean blue, white and a touch of raw umber. Decide on the positions of the motifs and attach the stencil to the wall using low-tack masking tape. Using only a very little paint on a stencilling brush, gently stroke in the shape. Repeat until the design is complete.

An intricate Chinoiserie stencil motif for walls. Complicated stencils hand cut from card or plastic can deteriorate quickly when used repeatedly so make sure you have a back-up copy.

Make sure you rest on a stable, protected surface or cutting board while using the knife, and try to cut in smooth, flowing movements or the clarity of the shape will be lost. Once you have reached the stencilling stage, the stencil should be stuck temporarily to the wall with either masking tape or a spray adhesive so that it will not become dislodged. The image should be created using gentle stippling or circular motions. The most important thing to remember when stencilling is to use a minute amount of paint on your brush and to blot even this out on newspaper before you start. The back of the stencil should be wiped occasionally to prevent any smudging.

Panelled door

Picking out decorative mouldings in a separate colour is an excellent way of breaking up large expanses of woodwork, such as the faces of fitted cupboards. Some people like to disguise them completely by papering over or painting them a colour identical to that of the walls, but I think if your cupboard door has original mouldings, they should be seen as an asset to make the most of.

When choosing your cupboard colour, it is safest to pick one that is going to reinforce an existing colour in your scheme. Here we mixed a lighter tone of the dusty blue used on the bedroom stool, which was also echoed in the stencilled walls. Rather like the grisaille method used to decorate the stool (see p.176), the simplest but most effective way of approaching the door is to work in three tones of the same colour but in a slightly different order from that used on the stool. The lightest tone was applied to the four inner panels, followed by a slightly darker tone for the surrounding frame and trim (architrave), and the darkest of all was used for the narrow beading containing each of the four panels. By using different tones in this way, you can emphasize the depth of the recessed panels which will, in turn, emphasize the three-dimensional solidity of the door.

The application employed was a dragging movement and the paint, a glaze mixed from water-based scumble and acrylic colours, which stays wet and workable for 10-15 minutes was put on using a dragging movement. It is best to follow the direction of the moulding when dragging – horizontal for the cross timbers and trim (architrave) top, and vertical for the four panels, vertical timbers and left- and right-hand sides of the trim (architrave). Dragging can be done with either regular brushes, varnish brushes or gliders, or even with floggers if you want a splintery, wood-like finish. Before starting it is a good idea to remove handles and any other fixtures from the area to be decorated as it is extremely difficult to keep straight lines around such features.

Make the most of cupboard doors by dragging the verticals and horizontals in soft colours and picking out the beading in slightly darker tones.

Our door originally came in a lime green gloss which was quickly dealt with a coat of acrylic primer which allowed the application of a different colour without the need for stripping (above).

MATERIALS AND EQUIPMENT

coarse-grade
sandpaper
(optional)

white satin
(eggshell) acrylic
paint

water

scumble glaze

acrylic primer
(optional)

paint brushes,
including a fitch, a
1½ in (40 mm)
brush, a wide
varnish brush and a
½ in (12 mm) flat-
ended brush

artist's acrylic paints
in cerulean blue,
white and raw
umber

satin (eggshell)
acrylic varnish

By picking out the mouldings in
a strong colour, the extensive
surface area of multiple built-in
units can be broken up and
given definition and elegance.

STEP 1 Prepare the door. If it has previously been painted in gloss paint, sand it down with coarse-grade sandpaper and then paint with an acrylic primer. When dry, apply a coat of white satin (eggshell) acrylic paint. Leave to dry thoroughly.

STEP 2 Using a fitch, mix 1 part water: 2 parts scumble glaze with artist's paints in cerulean blue, white and a dash of raw umber to create a watery coloured glaze.

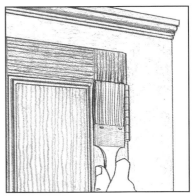

STEP 3 Create a dragged effect on the door panels by applying a thin coat of the watery glaze mixture using the 1½ in (40 mm) brush. Then drag downwards from top to bottom using a wide varnish brush. Darken the glaze slightly by adding more colour and paint the surrounding frame area, making sure that the left- and right-hand verticals cut cleanly across the top and bottom horizontals.

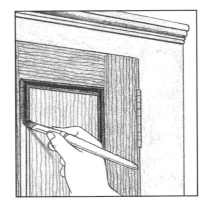

JOCASTA'S TIP

To add a pretty detail perfect for bedroom doors, try hanging a soft tassel in co-ordinating colours from the handle or key of the door. Tassels can be found in most department or haberdashery stores.

STEP 4 Make the glaze even darker and, using a ½ in (12 mm) flat-ended brush, pick out the beading around each panel. Do not make this colour too dark or it will overpower the gentle dragged effect. Leave to dry, then apply a coat of satin acrylic varnish.

Ribbons and bows stool

For those of you who like the look of delicately hand-painted furniture but are not so confident of your free-hand skills, transfer painting is the answer. Designs can be applied to furniture by using transfer paper. This comes in chalky sheets that behave rather like carbon paper but without the thick, black carbon which tends to smudge. Though quite expensive, transfer paper can be used again and again and comes in different colours which is a help when transferring designs onto different coloured backgrounds. There are many pattern source books available from art stores, but you could trace off designs from old magazines, design books, prints or fabrics. Once the shape is laid down you can then paint using acrylic paints and fine water-colour brushes of different sizes.

Delicate hand-painting can be fiddly, especially for a beginner. Preparation of the surface must be thorough – the smoother the base ground, the easier the brush strokes are to execute and the more clarity they will have. Filling and sanding, followed by two coats of ready-made acrylic gesso is the process recommended for really battered pieces. Mix acrylic colours with acrylic flow enhancer to give smoothness and fluency to strokes. Gum arabic performs the same function when mixed with gouache colours.

The design used here was painted in grisaille, a monochrome scheme based on light and dark shades of one colour. Using this simple but very effective method you can give a three-dimensional look to your motif, by first painting in the whole motif with a middle tone of your colour, going on to a darker one for the shadows and using a lighter, opaque one for the highlights. Once dry, the motifs will look more subtle if gently distressed with fine sandpaper and then washed over with a raw umber antiquing glaze.

pencil

coarse-grade sandpaper (optional)

acrylic primer (optional)

Baltic Blue Woodwash, or flat latex (matt emulsion) paint

paint brushes, including some water colour brushes

image pattern (this one is called "Ribbons and Bows")

tracing paper

low-tack masking tape

transfer paper

acrylic flow enhancer

fine-grade sandpaper

artist's acrylic paints in cobalt blue, Prussian blue, raw umber and white

soft rag

Antiquing Patina, or raw umber

satin acrylic varnish

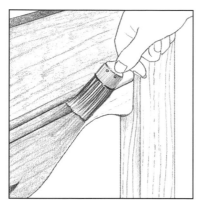

STEP 1 Prepare the stool. If it has previously been painted with gloss paint, sand it down using coarse-grade sandpaper and paint with a coat of acrylic primer and leave to dry. Apply a solid coat of Baltic Blue Woodwash or flat latex (matt emulsion) paint. Leave to dry.

STEP 2 Trace the selected design onto tracing paper. Transfer it to the painted surface by placing a sheet of transfer paper in the required position on the stool and then putting the tracing on top of this. Tape in place using low-tack masking tape and draw over the design using a soft pencil.

STEP 3 Mix some acrylic flow enhancer with artist's paints in cobalt blue and Prussian blue. Remove the transfer paper and paint in the design using water colour brushes. Mix some raw umber with the blue paint to create the shadows, and add some white to the blue for the highlights. Leave to dry.

STEP 4 Sand the design very lightly using fine-grade sandpaper and then antique the paintwork using a little raw umber mixed with acrylic varnish. Brush on this tint and wipe it off here and there using a soft rag. Allow it to collect in any recesses and then varnish with a satin acrylic varnish.

JOCASTA'S TIP

To create an immaculately smooth finish for painted furniture, apply three coats of oil-based satin varnish, sanding inbetween each coat with fine silicon carbide (wet-and-dry) paper. Polish the final coat with wax or boot polish.

Book door

In the bedroom a door hid an alcove storage area. The door had a modern, flush surface in heavy white gloss, and, to have a little fun, we decided to create an illusion of bookshelves laden with old tomes and paperbacks. A tradition that goes back a long way, book doors were a common device for concealing secret passageways or convenience areas, sometimes even using real book spines glued to the face of the door and the shelves created with horizontal strips of wooden beading. This is a clever trick but ripping up books is hard to justify and a rather shameful exercise. The next best thing, which works very successfully, is to make colour photocopies of the spines. You can make interesting arrangements with the spines, some upright, some lying flat, others leaning against each other. Even if you only manage to find a few spines to colour copy, these can be repeated over and over. Once in place all sorts of trickery can be achieved by adding a few genuine articles such as postcards or invitations.

It is best to glue the copies to a dark background in a colour such as raw umber or dark green so that these areas recede like shadows. The door frame and the face of the shelves themselves should be painted in a light colour, preferably the same one used for the woodwork in the rest of the room. The sharp horizontal shelf fronts can be achieved by using a level and masking tape. If any of the woodwork in the rest of the room is unpainted, i.e., showing the grain, then you could try to match this with some simple woodgraining.

If you want to try some *trompe-l'œil* you could paint in some book spines by hand. Transfer paper could be used to create the lettering of the title and gold paints used for imitating gold tooled work. Making up titles and painting in a few of your own is great fun and a good way of introducing family jokes.

MATERIALS AND EQUIPMENT

coarse-grade sandpaper (optional)

acrylic primer (optional)

dark green flat latex (matt emulsion) paint

paint brushes

pencil

tape measure or ruler

spirit level

low-tack masking tape

cream flat latex (matt emulsion) paint

water

wide varnish brush

colour photocopies of book spines

scissors

PVA glue

flat (matt) acrylic vanish

A very plain and unremarkable door (above). After sanding and priming the surface we decided to transform it into a "book shelf" with a few clever tricks.

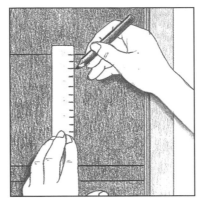

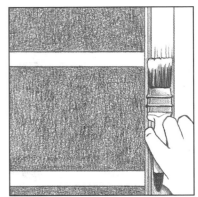

STEP 1 If the door has previously been painted with gloss paint, sand it down using coarse-grade sandpaper, and apply a coat of acrylic primer. Allow to dry, then apply a base coat of dark green flat latex (matt emulsion) paint. Leave to dry.

STEP 2 To create the "shelves", measure 1 in (2.5 cm) thick horizontal bands at regular intervals down the length of the door. Try to leave at least 12 in (30 cm) gaps between each shelf, but this may depend on the total height available. Put strips of low-tack masking tape above and below the shelf fronts, using a spirit level to ensure they are straight.

STEP 3 Paint the "shelf fronts" using cream flat latex (matt emulsion) and continue in this colour around the door frame to emphasize the "built-in" look. Leave to dry, then dilute the dark green paint with water and, using a wide varnish brush, drag this tint over the cream to soften it.

JOCASTA'S TIP

If the door you are decorating has a prominent handle that spoils the *trompe-l'œil* effect, try replacing it with a small glass one.

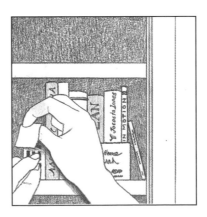

STEP 4 Cut out the colour photocopies and work out the arrangement of books on each shelf. Stick them to the door using PVA glue. Make sure the edges of the books are well glued otherwise they may curl in time. When the design is complete, seal the whole door with a coat of flat (matt) acrylic varnish.

We created the illusion of a book shelf by applying colour photocopies of book spines.

The decorator's organizer

Use our Decorator's Organizer to plan your projects. Photocopy the charts as many times as you require, and the pages can then be used repeatedly. They will help you avoid wasted trips to suppliers by allowing you to record details of each room in the designated boxes. Attach swatches, magazine cuttings and paint colour lists, and jot down any ideas that occur while you are planning. This collection of information should also help you to keep an eye on expenses.

Preliminary Information

ROOM:
DECORATION PROJECT:
INTENDED COLOUR SCHEME:
DIMENSIONS OF ROOM:

Decorating company Contact name: Telephone: Price quoted: Further budget for materials
Commencement date:
Completion date:

	WALLS	CEILINGS	FLOORS	WOODWORK
Surface area				
Preparation: Current material				
State of repair				
Preparation work				
Dates for preparation				
Paint Effect: Chosen paint effect				
Dates for paint effects				
Materials: Paint names/colours				
Brand & code no.				
Recipe (if a mix)				
Finishing				
To Hire:				
To Buy:				
Suppliers:				
Colour Swatch Boxes				

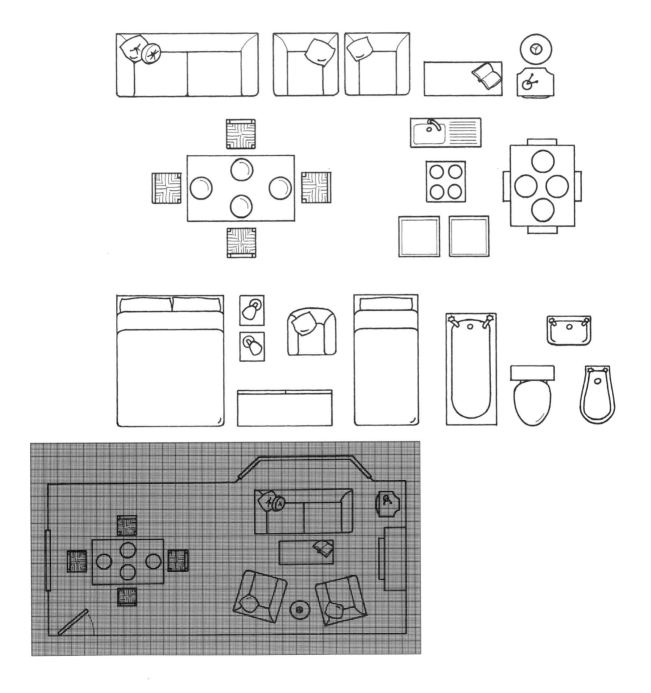

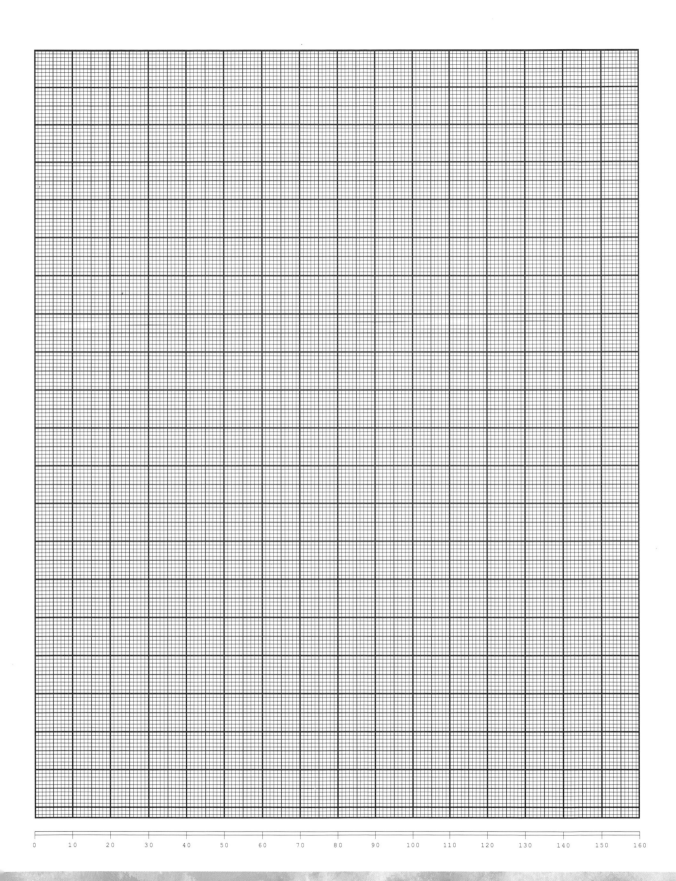

0   10   20   30   40   50   60   70   80   90   100   110   120   130   140   150   160

	TO KEEP	TO REVAMP	TO BUY
Fixtures			

Lighting: Main
      Secondary
      Switches			

Doors: Handles Plates			
Windows: Locks			
Radiators			

Fireplace: Mantle
    Grate
    Hearth			

Accessories			
Curtains/Blinds Tie backs			
Rugs/Carpets			
Cushions			
Lamps			
Painting/Prints			
Mirrors			
Stockists:		**Budget:**	

Glossary

Acetate Transparent plastic film that can be used for cutting stencils. It is tough and particularly good at bending around corners. Its transparency allows for the registration of the design.

Acrylic Convertor A water-based acrylic primer produced by Paint Magic that works particularly well on laminated surfaces such as melamine or Formica enabling you to apply any decorative paint effect.

Acrylic gesso Ready-made, synthetic gesso for priming surfaces for further decoration.

Acrylic primer Made up of acrylic polymers, acrylic primer has a high degree of white pigment and is a high-build paint designed to be painted over. In most cases it eliminates the need for an undercoat. Several coats can make a cheap alternative to acrylic gesso.

All-purpose cleaner Also known as sugar soap. A degreasing agent used to wash down surfaces before painting.

Aluminium oxide paper A type of abrasive paper for preparing surfaces.

Architrave See Trim.

Badger-hair softener The finest brush for softening purposes. Made from real badger hair secured in a wooden handle, it is most commonly used for blending oil- and water-based glazes in the techniques of marbling and woodgraining.

Baseboards The wooden trim applied to the bottom of interior walls to protect them from wear.

Simple shapes lend themselves to brilliant colour. Let colour make a statement about you.

Beeswax A natural wax produced from the honeycombs of bees. Yellowish in colour but transparent in use, beeswax is used as a protective finish for wood and comes in liquid, solid or pellet form.

Broken colour A term referring to the use of transparent glazes applied to surfaces where the means of application, i.e., sponge or rag, is visible, rather than forming a solid, opaque coat.

Carbon paper Thin film coated in black carbon normally used for duplication in typing. Can also be used for transferring motifs onto stencil card or surfaces to be decorated.

Carnauba wax A natural wax derived from a Brazilian palm leaf. It is the hardest of all waxes, has a very high melting point and polishes to an exceptionally high degree.

Chinoiserie Oriental-inspired decorative motifs.

Chipboard Sheets of board made up of coarse compressed wood chips; used in structural work.

Colourwash A water-based, transparent glaze or diluted latex (emulsion) designed to create a fresco-like finish for walls. Some companies produce ready-mixed colourwashes, such as Paint Magic Colourwash; these have an in-built retardant to slow their drying time and so enabling easy application.

Complementary colour These are colours that when added together in equal proportions produce a neutral shade; they are found on opposite points of a colour wheel e.g. yellow and blue, red and orange.

Cornicing Applied plaster decoration where walls meet ceiling.

Crackle glaze A sticky, water-based medium applied underneath latex (emulsion) paints to cause them to crack. Best used between two different coloured latex (emulsion) paints. A hairdrier can be used to accelerate the cracking effect of the top coat of paint.

Craft knife Small, sharp knife suitable for cutting stencils and other decorative equipment. Blades, which are available in different shapes and sizes, should be changed regularly.

Craquelure An antiquing effect, craquelure is the fine cracking of varnish caused by a fast-drying varnish being applied over a slow-drying varnish making the top one split. Oil paint is rubbed into the cracks to make them more prominent. Craquelure works particularly well over découpage. Some companies produce ready-to-go twin packs of craquelure varnishes while some artists use standard water- and oil-based varnishes.

Découpage The application of prints or paper scraps to furniture or decorative objects.

Denatured alcohol (methylated spirit) Unrefined alcohol used as a solvent for spirit-based materials and shellacs. In Britain it is tinted purple, in the US it is clear. Can be used for stripping old shellacs or cleaning glass.

Distemper A traditional, water-based paint made from whiting, rabbit-skin glue and pigments. The finish is flat (matt) and chalky but should not be powdery if properly mixed.

Dragging A scumble-glaze effect for furniture and woodwork created by holding the bristles of a dragging or varnish brush close to a surface that has been given a layer of glaze. The brush is dragged vertically or horizontally to leave fine stripes of glaze.

Dusting brush A versatile brush that has soft, medium length bristles set in a wooden handle. Can be used for stippling on a small scale or for softening glaze work, though the bristles are not as fine as a badger hair softener.

Dutch metal leaf A cheaper alternative to true gold leaf, Dutch metal leaf comes in books of 25 leaves, loose or backed by waxed paper. Unlike true gold leaf, Dutch metal tarnishes and so must be sealed with varnish of shellac. Gilding size is used to apply it to the surface and with clever antiquing methods Dutch metal can look as effective as true gold leaf.

Eggshell See Mid-sheen or satin paint.

Emulsion See Latex.

Flogger This is primarily a wood-graining brush. It has long flexible horse hair bristles which are flicked against wet glaze to create a woody, fibrous texture.

Flow enhancer A liquid medium for water-based paints such as artist's acrylics that eases their application with the brush.

Fitches A rounded, long-handled brush with flexible but firm bristles suitable for mixing paint colours and other materials. Fitches are available in different sizes and because of their domed end are suitable for stencilling also.

Formica See Laminates.

French polish Shellac-based lacquer that is derived from seedlac, animal resin, dissolved in alcohol

(methylated spirits) and heated to produce a rich, dark protective finish for wood. French polish is applied to wood using a ''rubber'', a wad of rags soaked in the medium.

Gesso A material traditionally used for preparing the surface of furniture or decorative panels for gilding. Rabbit-skin glue is melted and dissolved in hot water and whiting added to create a thick, white medium. Gesso has a very good filling capacity and multiple layers, sanded down in between with fine sandpaper will produce an immaculately smooth finish for further decoration.

Gilt cream/wax Metallic powders suspended in a turpentine-based wax make a rich decorative material perfect for metallic highlights or touching in old gilded work. Gilt creams dry to a hard finish which can be buffed with a rag.

Glider A light brush, with thin, silky bristles perfect for varnishing, applying shellac or glazes.

Graining The imitation of natural wood grain using tinted glazes and specially designed brushes such as floggers and over-grainers. Graining is most commonly achieved using oil-based scumble glazes but water-based paints as well as vinegar and powder pigment are also used.

Grisaille A monochrome version of *trompe-l'œil.* Three-dimensional shapes such as decorative mouldings are created on flat surfaces using different shades of one colour.

Gum arabic A form of naturally produced gum that is water-based and available in liquid or crystal form. It can be used as a medium for water colour and gouache paints as well as a delicate glue.

Impasto paint A thick, textured, water-based paint produced by Paint Magic that can be used to create wall effects ranging from soft distressing to high-build textured finishes.

Japan paint Originally produced in the nineteenth century to imitate oriental lacquer, this paint has a glossy, hard finish and is made from pigment suspended in an oil-free varnish or enamel.

Japan wax A natural wax extracted from the berries of the sumac tree, which is very oily and tough.

Knotting A shellac-based material used to seal knots in new wood to prevent paintwork being stained with leaking sap.

Lacquering Genuine lacquer is made from resin obtained from the orishi tree found in Japan and China. It is produced by the *Cocca lacca* insect which penetrates the bark of the tree and desposits the lac which is the raw material for lacquer. It is then thickened through evaporation and coloured with pigments. Multiple coats are applied to objects and sanded thoroughly in between to create a hard, smooth, shiny surface ideal for carving, gilding or inlay. Nowadays shellacs, varnishes or gloss paints are used to imitate the look.

Laminates Tough surface material formed by pressing together layers of different substances. Most commonly used to clad kitchen units and countertops. Comes in different forms such as Formica or melamine.

Latex Water-based paint made up from pigments and synthetic resins, usually PVA or acrylic polymers, dispersed in water to form a binder. This is the quickest, cheapest and fastest drying finish for walls and ceilings. Easily obtainable, can be tinted with universal stainers and acrylics.

Limewash A traditional paint made from slaked lime, pigment, animal glue and water. Its great advantage over modern paints is that it allows the wall to breathe, and water and salts from the wall to pass through. It does not peel and crack like plastic paints.

Liming A traditional and classic finish where limewash is diluted and applied to furniture. Real lime is caustic so the material also provides protection against bacteria. A modern and tougher equivalent can be made by mixing white pigment with beeswax and rubbing onto woodwork. The most suitable woods are those that have a definite grain, such as oak and ash. Some companies produce a paste version e.g. Paint Magic Liming Paste.

Liner or lining paper A thick paper used for lining walls before painting or wallpapering. It will cover cracks or rough surfaces and is applied with a paste adhesive.

Lining brush A brush designed specifically for the creation of straight lines for furniture decoration. Long, soft bristles enable the brush to carry more paint so that the line need not be broken repeatedly to take up more colour.

Linseed oil A natural oil obtained from the seeds of the flax plant. Boiled linseed oil is used for fine painting, and raw linseed oil for exterior work.

Marbelizing The imitation of marble using glazes and specialist brushes. Oil-based scumble glazes are most commonly used as they remain wet and therefore workable for some time. Feathers and fine brushes are used for creating veins and badger hair softeners for blending the effect.

Masking tape A very useful tape essential to any decorator. Masking tape is low-tack and so will not pull paint from a surface. It can be used to mask off areas when applying a finish to selected areas only, for creating straight lines on decorative work and for sticking things temporarily to surfaces.

Melamine A laminated material usually used in the construction of kitchen units and other modern furniture (see Laminates).

Methylated spirits See Denatured alcohol.

Mid-sheen or satin paint Oil-based paint that has a slight sheen. It has the consistency of cream and dries to a smooth, hard, opaque surface that is non-porous, suitable for furniture and interior woodwork, as well as a base paint for oil-based scumble glaze work.

Paint thinner A solvent for oil-based products; a cheaper alternative to turpentine.

Papier-mâché A modelling material made from shredded paper and water-based glues such as wallpaper adhesive. Papier-mâché dries hard and can be decorated with paints, gilding and other finishes.

Pigment Pigments are finely ground solids suspended in binder and used for colouring materials. They are obtained from the earth, from minerals and from plants.

Polyvinyl acetate A synthetic resin used extensively in latex (emulsion) paint produced by the polymerization of vinyl acetate.

Plumb line Pointed weight on the end of a cord, suspended to determine a true vertical.

Plywood Thin wooden sheets glued together with the grain in alternate directions to form a strong but springy board.

PVA (polyvinyl acrylic) A very versatile material, polyvinyl acrylic can be used as a sealer, binder or glue.

Rabbit-skin glue Glue obtained from the skin of rabbits, available in granule or sheet form. This is melted in hot water and added to whiting to make gesso. As it is organic the glue will eventually decay if left in its wet form.

Ragging The decorative paint effect achieved by pressing or rolling a cotton rag in wet glaze. Ragging is sometimes used as one of the first processes of marbling.

Red oxide metal primer A dark red coloured, oil-based primer that prevents rusting.

Rotten stone A grey coloured powder that can be mixed with oil to polish surfaces, or mixed with shellac to create a dark, antiquing patina for gilding. Rotten stone can also be dusted on dry using a soft brush to imitate the build up of dust in decorative mouldings.

Scumble glaze This is a transparent medium into which colour and solvent are mixed to create glaze for techniques such as stippling, ragging, marbling and wood-graining. Oil-based scumble glaze is made from linseed oil, driers and resins, acrylic scumble from acrylic resin.

Shavehook See Triangular scraper.

Shellac A quick-drying lacquer derived from shellac, an animal resin, which is cleaned, crushed and dissolved in alcohol and applied traditionally to woodwork to stain and seal it leaving a smooth surface.

Shellac is heated to produce darker shades such as french, garnet or button polish. It can be used as a sealer inbetween layers of decorative work, or as a medium for metallic powders. Its solvent is denatured alcohol (methylated spirit).

Silicon carbide paper Also known as wet-and-dry paper. Fine sandpaper which is particularly good for sanding down existing paintwork to create a "key" for subsequent coats of paint to grip onto. It can be dipped in water first; this prevents the paper from becoming clogged with fine particles.

Size Alternative term for glue or sealer. Size can be made from synthetic or organic materials and have different setting times.

Skirting boards See Baseboards.

Snagging The finishing up of decorative techniques.

Softening The action using the tips of a soft bristled brush, such as a badger hair softener, to soften and blend decorative effects including marbling and wood graining.

Solvent A material used to dissolve substances such as grime or old paint.

Spackle (filler) Used to fill cracks and holes, particularly in plaster.

Sponging A technique that uses a synthetic or natural sponge to apply colour to a surface or take colour off, leaving an impression of the surface of the sponge.

Stain A coloured substance used to tint materials such as wood or fabric, resulting in a transparent finish. Stains can be oil-, spirit- or water-based.

Stencilling The technique of applying decorative motifs to a surface using patterns cut from card or acetate. Paint is "pounced" or dabbed on through the stencil using a specially designed stencil brush.

Stippling A decorative finish for flat surfaces such as walls and furniture that is achieved by "pouncing" the tips of bristles into wet glaze leaving pin pricks of colour.

Stripper Caustic paste or liquid containing methylene chloride that can be used to dissolve layers of old paint or varnish that are then scraped off with a wire brush or triangular scraper (shavehook).

Sugar soap See All-purpose cleaner.

Tile primer An oil-based paint that can be applied to ceramic and other non-porous surfaces to prepare them for the application of further finishes. This type of primer stays soft and flexible which prevents it from being chipped off easily.

Titanium dioxide A dense, opaque white pigment which is the main ingredient of household paint. It acts as a filler, adding bulk to the paint, making it cheaper to produce. Titanium also increases the brightness of paint as it scatters light.

Triangular scraper A metal tool used to scrape paint from flat or curved surfaces, specially useful on mouldings.

Trim Applied decorative mouldings making up a door frame.

Trompe-L'Œil
This term, meaning "to deceive the eye", refers to the use of paints to create the illusion of three-dimensional objects on a flat surface.

Transfer paper A thin paper backed on one side with coloured chalk that can be used to transfer designs onto surfaces by placing it over photocopied designs and pressing through with a pencil.

Turpentine The usual solvent for oil-based products. Paint thinner (white spirit) is a cheaper imitation of turpentine.

Verdigris The patination of metals such as copper, bronze or brass caused by the corrosive action of air and sea water over time, producing a green, powdery coating. Imitated as a paint effect using different shades of green latex (emulsion) stippled on with a soft stencilling brush.

Wet-and-dry paper See Silicon carbide paper.

White spirit See Paint thinner.

Whiting Natural calcium carbonate ground to a fine powder; used to make gesso and traditional paints such as distemper.

Woodchip paper Cheap, textured wallpaper suitable for concealing rough or damaged walls.

Woodwash A thick, water-based paint manufactured by Paint Magic that can be used as transparent wash for new wood, as a rich opaque coat or to produce distressed finishes. It contains a thickener which allows the paint to be burnished once dry with wire wool creating a rich, antique sheen. Flat latex (emulsion) paint can also be used.

Stockists

Paint Magic Branches:
Paint Magic offers a complete range of decorative paints, brushes, stencils, books and videos. Each branch also offers weekly courses in decorative paint techniques and a design and decoration service.

Britain

Head Office, Shop and Mail order
116 Sheen Road
Richmond, Surrey
TW9 1UR
Tel: 0181 940 5503
Fax: 0181 332 7503

5 Elgin Crescent,
London W11 2JR
Tel: 0171 792 8012
Fax: 0171 727 0207

26 High Street,
Arundel, West Sussex
Tel: 0903 883653
Fax: 0903 884367

North America

2426 Fillmore St,
San Francisco, CA 94115,
USA
Tel: 415 292 7780
Fax: 415 292 7782

Paint Magic products are also available at Pottery Barn stores around the country

Canada

101, 1019 17th Avenue S.W.
Calgary,
Alberta T2T 0A7, Canada

Singapore

30 Watten Rise, Singapore,
1128.

Other suppliers:

We would like to thank many of the following companies for the very kind loan of merchandise.

Specialist paints and equipment:

Stuart Stevenson
68 Clerkenwell Road,
London EC1M 5QA
Tel: 0171 253 1693

Green & Stone
259 Kings Road,
London SW3 5ER
Tel: 0171 352 0837

A. S. Handover
Angel Yard, Highgate
High Street,
London N6 5JU
Tel: 0171 359 4696
Fax: 0171 354 3658

For historic colours in water and oil:

Craig & Rose
172 Leith Walk,
Edinburgh EH6 5EB
Tel: 0131 554 1131

Farrow & Ball
33 Uddens Trading Estate,
Wimbourne, Dorset
BH21 7NL
Tel: 0202 876141
Fax: 0202 873793

Papers & Paints
4 Park Walk,
London SW10 0AD
Tel: 0171 352 8626
Fax: 0171 352 1017

Specialist restoration products, varnishes, waxes and shellacs:

John Myland Ltd
80 Norwood High Street,
London SE27 9NW
Tel: 0181 670 9161
Fax: 0181 761 5700

Conservation supplies:

Jane Schofield
Lewdon Farm, Black Dog,
Crediton, Devon
EX17 4QQ
Tel: 0884 8611181

Hirst Conservation
Materials Ltd
Laughton, Sleaford,
Lincolnshire NG34 0HE
Tel: 0529 7517
Fax: 0529 7518

Source books and stencils:

Hillbury Press
Cranbourne Industrial
Estate,
Cranbourne Road,
Potters Bar,
Herts EN6 3JN
Tel: 0707 658 748

The Dover Bookshop
35 Earlham Street,
London WC2 9PJ
Tel: 0171 836 2111

Decorative furniture and other accessories:

Graham & Green
4 Elgin Crescent,
London W11 2JA
Tel: 0171 727 4594
Kitchen p.133: galvanized cider urn, yellow bowl, tea towels, kitchen utensils.
Bathroom p.149: cushions, mosaic bowl with shells, mirror with candles, rug, tooth mug.

The Blue Door
77 Church Road,
London SW13 9HH
Tel: 0181 748 9785
Bedroom p.165: bedspreads and cushions, pewter wall sconces, half-moon table, blue cupboard, shell prints, rugs.

David Wainwright
251 Portobello Road,
London W11 1LT
Tel: 0171 792 1988
Sitting room p.115: mirror, coffee table, central light, decorative statues. Kitchen p.115: iron pot hanger.

Highly Sprung
185-186 Tottenham Court Road, London W1P 9LE
Tel: 0171 631 1424
Sitting room p.115: sofa and armchair in Malabar fabric.

The Reject Shop (branches around the UK): Kitchen p.133: bread bin, apron.

Paperchase
213 Tottenham Court Road, London W1P 9AF.
Sitting room p.115: nut garland and nugget bowl.

Spur Shelving
Spur Shelving, Spur House, Otterspool Way, Watford, Herts, WD2 8HT. Tel: 0923 226071.
Sitting room p.115: oak shelves.

Bed Discount Centre
52 Manor Road, London W13. Tel: 0181 997 3092.
Bedroom p.165: Pine framed Lay-easy Bed.

Mr Christians: Delicatessen
11 Elgin Crescent, London W11 2JA. Tel: 0171 229 0501. Kitchen p.133: food stuffs.

Index

Picture credits
The pictures that appear in the book
were obtained from the following
sources:

Abode UK – pp20, 25 (top), 26, 29, 56,
119
Jan Baldwin/Robert Harding Picture
Library – pp 36, 69, 99
Tim Beddow/Robert Harding Picture
Library – p102
Charlie Colmer/International Interiors –
p31
Mark Gatehouse/Paint Magic – pp1, 3, 7,
8, 9, 42-3, 50-1, 54-5, 57, 58-9, 60-1, 62-3,
65, 66-7, 76-7. 84-5, 86-7, 90-1, 105, 116,
151
Brian Harrison/Robert Harding Picture
Library – p47
Simon Kenny/Belle/Arcaid – p184
Country Living – p24
Carl Lyttle/Paint Magic – p30
James Merrell/Robert Harding Picture
Library – pp40, 41, 162
Paint Magic – pp137, 146, 169
Jonathan Pilkington/Robert Harding
Picture Library – p34
Paul Ryan/International Interiors – pp18,
33
Schulenberg/The Interior World –
pp106, 159
Lucinda Symons/Paint Magic – pp2, 10,
12-13, 14-15, 79, 114, 115, 117, 120, 124,
125, 127, 128, 129, 132, 133, 134, 138, 139,
143, 144, 145, 148, 149, 153, 154, 156, 160,
161, 164, 165, 167, 174, 175
Pia Tryde/Robert Harding Picture
Library – p96
Mark Luscombe White/Robert Harding
Picture Library – p22
Elizabeth Whiting Associates – pp6, 17,
23, 25 (bottom), 28, 35, 39, 100, 101, 172,
189